FIONA GOBLE

KNIT YOUR OWN
ZOMBIE

over **1000** COMBINATIONS to
RIP'N'REASSEMBLE for HORRIFYING RESULTS

Ivy Press

First published in the UK in 2012 by
Ivy Press
210 High Street
Lewes
East Sussex BN7 2NS
United Kingdom
www.ivypress.co.uk

British Library Cataloguing-in-Publication
Data. A catalogue record for this book is
available from the British Library

ISBN: 978-1-908005-48-9

This book was conceived,
designed and produced by
Ivy Press
Creative Director Peter Bridgewater
Publisher Susan Kelly
Commissioning Editor Sophie Collins
Editorial Director Tom Kitch
Art Director James Lawrence
Designer Clare Barber
Photographer Andrew Perris

Printed in China

Colour origination by Ivy Press
Reprographics

10 9 8 7 6 5 4 3 2 1

Important safety information
Many of the knitted figures are
small or have removable parts,
making them a choking hazard.
They are not suitable for children
under the age of 36 months.

CONtENTs

THE ZOMBIES

INTRODUCTION

When knits go wrong, things can turn very bad indeed. This book offers you eight horrible zombie characters, every one with his or her unique accoutrements, and all chillingly simple to knit. And there's something even better: every part of every zombie is rip'n'grip – heads and limbs are attached to the body using Velcro, so you can tear them apart like a toddler in a tantrum, then reassemble them in any way you want to create brand-new creations, unique to you.

You'll find that ripping the head off one of these little horrors is strangely therapeutic – once a knitted zombie has taken up residence on your desk, those tiresome executive toys will be a thing of the past. You can dispense with that rubbery stress ball or the ill-judged book on mindfulness meditation. Just tear up a zombie for an immediate lift.

There's a veritable smorgasbord of choices, too. From Zombie Cop to Frankenstein's Monster, each of the eight characters has his or her own outfit, accessories – and body parts. Start with Classic Zombie – he (or is it she?) is straightforward enough. Then make a pair, or three, or four . . . Mix and match their accessories as well as their limbs and heads: see how Zombie Gravedigger looks holding her own skull under her arm, but wearing someone else's head. However you mix them, there will always be other enticing combinations you can try.

Your WOrk BOX

You only need some basic tools and materials to get started on your knitted zombies. But it's a good idea to check through your work box before you begin to make sure that you've got everything you need.

KNITTING NEEDLES

The projects in this book are knitted using a pair of size 3 mm (US 2/3) standard knitting needles. To complete some projects, you will need a pair of size 2.75 mm (US 2) knitting needles too. The needles you need for each project are listed in the individual sections.

CROCHET HOOK

While the patterns do not involve actual crochet, a crochet hook in size 3.25 mm (US D-3) is required to create crochet chains that are used for some of the details. Full instructions are given within the patterns. If you already have a similarly but not identically sized crochet hook, it will be ok.

YARN NEEDLE

You will need a sewing needle with a large eye and a fairly blunt end to sew your work together. Sometimes these needles are called yarn needles, but a tapestry needle will work just as well.

EMBROIDERY NEEDLE

You will need an embroidery needle with a sufficiently large eye to thread through a length of DK yarn for embroidering the zombies' features and markings. These needles have more pointed ends than tapestry needles, allowing you to get between the strands of your yarn, which is crucial for working some stitches.

STANDARD SEWING NEEDLE

You will need an ordinary sewing needle to sew on the fastenings and some of the decorations, such as buttons and beads.

WATER-SOLUBLE PEN

This is useful to mark the position of the dolls' features and markings before you stitch them. Water-soluble pens are like ordinary felt pens, but the ink disappears when sprayed or dabbed with water. The ink is safe to use on almost all yarns and fabrics, but it is worth testing beforehand to make sure.

STITCH HOLDER

These are useful to hold spare stitches while you are working on a separate part of your knitting. You could also use a spare needle or large safety pins for this, since the projects are small.

PENCIL

You will need this to draw round the templates to create some of the zombies' accessories – an ordinary pencil is fine.

GREEN & GREY CRAYONS

These are used to colour some of the zombies' flesh – particularly the areas round the eyes.

SMALL SCISSORS

A pair of small, sharp scissors is vital for trimming yarn tails without the risk of cutting your knitting.

HOUSEHOLD SCISSORS

You will need these to cut out your card templates for a few of the zombie accessories.

JEWELLER'S PLIERS

These will be useful to add the jump rings to any charms you use and to create the handcuffs for the Zombie Cop.

TAPE MEASURE

You will need this to check the positioning of some of the fastenings and for measuring the length of your crochet chains. You may also need it to measure your yarns.

Yarns & Other StUFF YoU NEED

To make the projects in this book, you will need a selection of standard DK (double knitting) yarn. To make some of the clothes, hair and accessories, you will also need some special types of yarn. These and a few other essential materials are all mentioned here.

YARNS

The main parts of all the projects in the book are knitted in standard DK yarns. We recommend that you use 100 per cent wool yarns or yarns that contain at least 20 per cent wool. Yarns made from 100 per cent acrylic or 100 per cent cotton do not have the natural stretch of wool-based yarns and the results can be disappointing.

For some of the clothes, you will also need some special-effect DK yarn. For other items you will need sock yarn or 4-ply yarn, both of which are thinner than DK yarn and widely available. Some of the hair is created using mohair yarn or a yarn made from a mix of mohair and silk, which is a light, fluffy yarn and ideal for recreating wispy, zombie-like hair. For a few of the accessories, you will also need small amounts of dark silver metallic crochet yarn. All the yarns are listed in the 'You will need' section for the individual projects and can be bought from your local knitting shop.

STANDARD SEWING THREAD

You will need this to sew the fastenings to your projects and to sew on the buttons and beads. You do not need a variety of colours – all the projects in the book use cream sewing thread only.

POLYESTER TOY FILLING

This is a soft, fluffy filling made from 100 per cent polyester that is specially made to stuff toys and hand-crafted items. It is widely available in craft shops. Make sure that the one you choose conforms to all relevant safety standards.

VELCRO FASTENING TAPE

The main zombie body parts are joined together with Velcro, allowing you to dismember your doll and mix and match components from different zombie dolls. Make sure you buy the sew-in version of the tape (rather than the self-adhesive or iron-on versions) and choose a colour that most closely matches your doll. The tape is normally available in white and black, but you can also buy it in beige in some craft shops.

SNAP FASTENERS

Each zombie's arms are joined to the body using 13 mm (½ in) snap fasteners. You can buy these from a craft or haberdashery shop.

BUTTONS & BEADS

To create some of the zombies' teeth, fingernails and accessories, you will need a few buttons, beads, brads and bows. Check out what you can find in your work box before you buy something specially. You do not need to use exactly the same types that we show in the project – sometimes you can discover a great look when you are least expecting it by experimenting a bit.

PLASTIC DRINKING STRAWS

These are used to create some of the zombie accessories.

SILVER OR GREY CARD

You will need a small amount of this to make the templates for some of the zombie accessories.

CHARMS

A few of the zombies have special jewellery created from spooky metal charms. These are available in some craft and bead shops or from online suppliers.

A FEW EXTRAS

One or two of the projects require some less usual but still widely available items such as metal rings, waxed cord and lengths of jewellery-making chain. Check out the 'You will need' section in the individual projects to discover what you need for each zombie.

ABBREVIATIONS

You will find the following knitting abbreviations in this book.

K	knit
P	purl
st(s)	stitch(es)
st st	stocking stitch
beg	beginning
k2tog	knit the next 2 stitches together
p2tog	purl the next 2 stitches together
kwise	by knitting the stitch or stitches
pwise	by purling the stitch or stitches
inc1	increase one stitch by knitting into the front and then the back of the next stitch
M1	make one stitch by picking up the horizontal loop before the next stitch and knitting into the back of it.
s1	slip one (slip a stitch onto the right-hand needle without knitting it)
psso	pass slipped stitch over (pass the slipped stitch over the stitch just knitted)
ssk	slip, slip, knit (slip 2 stitches, one at a time, then knit the slipped stitches together)
RS	right side
WS	wrong side
yf	yarn forward (bring your yarn from the back to the front of your work)
cont	continue
rem	remaining
rep	repeat
g	gram
oz	ounce
mm	millimetre
cm	centimetre
in	inch
m	metre
ft	foot
yd	yard

TENSION

The knitting tension for the patterns in this book is 12 sts and 16 rows to 4 cm (1½ in) square over st st on 3 mm (US 2/3) needles.

The tension when knitting small items like the ones in this book is not normally as crucial as when you are knitting clothes. The main thing is to make sure that your knitting is quite firm, so that your items keep their shape and the stuffing does not show through the knitted fabric. However, if you knit unusually tightly, you may want to use slightly larger needles than recommended. If you knit loosely, you may want to choose slightly smaller knitting needles.

The Guts of The Matter

All knitting is made up from two basic stitches – the knit stitch and the purl stitch. You'll also need to know how to cast on and cast off. If you want to refresh your memory for knitting basics before you begin, you're in the right place. For a few of the projects, you'll need to know a couple of intermediate techniques: lace-effect knitting and knitting with two colours at once.

CASTING ON

1 Make a slip knot by making a simple loop of yarn and pulling another loop of yarn through it. Insert your needle through the loop and pull the slip knot up quite firmly. This is your first cast-on stitch.

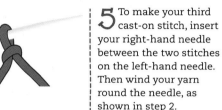

2 To make the next cast-on stitch, hold the needle with the slip knot in your left hand. Insert the point of your right-hand needle through the slip knot from left to right. Wind your yarn round the needle tip.

3 Use the tip of your needle to pull a loop of yarn through the first cast-on stitch. You now have your second cast-on stitch.

4 Transfer the new stitch to the left-hand needle.

5 To make your third cast-on stitch, insert your right-hand needle between the two stitches on the left-hand needle. Then wind your yarn round the needle, as shown in step 2.

6 Use the tip of your needle to pull a loop of yarn through the gap between the stitches, and then transfer this new stitch to your left-hand needle.

Repeat the last two steps until you have the number of stitches you need.

KNITTING

1 Insert your right-hand needle from left to right, into the front of the first stitch to be knitted.

2 Wind your yarn round the needle, from left to right.

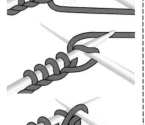

3 Use the tip of your needle to draw a loop of yarn through the stitch. This is your new stitch.

4 Pull your right hand needle gently to the right, so that the original stitch comes off the left-hand needle.

Repeat these steps until you have knitted all your stitches. To get ready for the next row, put the needle with all the stitches into your left hand.

PURLING

This is like working a knit stitch in reverse.

1 With your yarn at the front of your work, insert your right-hand needle from right to left into the front of the first stitch that is on your left-hand needle.

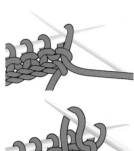

2 Wind your yarn round the tip of your needle, from top to bottom.

3 Use the tip of your needle to pull a loop of yarn through the original stitch. This is your new stitch.

4 Pull your right-hand needle gently to the right, so that the original stitch comes off the left-hand needle.

Repeat these steps until you have purled all the stitches on the left-hand needle. To get ready for the next row, put the needle with all the stitches into your left hand.

CAST OFF KNITWISE

1 Knit two stitches in the normal way. With the tip of your left-hand needle, lift the first stitch you have knitted over the second knitted stitch.

2 Knit the next stitch so that there are two stitches on your needle again, and repeat step 1.

Continue in this way until you have just one stitch left. Trim the yarn, leaving a fairly long tail that can be used for sewing your item together, and then pull your last stitch through.

CAST OFF PURLWISE

This is just like casting off knitwise, but you purl the stitches instead of knitting them.

1 Purl two stitches in the normal way. With the tip of your left-hand needle, lift the first stitch you have purled over the second purled stitch.

2 Purl the next stitch so that you have two stitches on your needle again, and repeat step 1.

Continue in this way until you have just one stitch left. Trim the yarn, leaving a fairly long tail that can be used for sewing your item together, and then pull your last stitch through.

COMBINING KNIT & PURL STITCHES

When you knit every row, the knitted fabric that you produce is called garter stitch.

When you work alternate rows of knit and purl stitches, the knitted fabric that you produce is called stocking or stockinette stitch, which is the main stitch used for the projects in this book.

When you work vertical rows of knit and purl stitches by combining the two stitches in one row, the knitted fabric that you produce is called ribbing or rib stitch.

LACE-EFFECT KNITTING

This is created by working a combination of knit and purl stitches and a special stitch that involves taking your yarn from the back to the front of your work (written in the patterns as yf or yarn forward) and then knitting two stitches together. The loop that is created from taking your yarn to the front of your work creates an additional stitch.

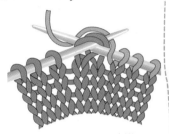

KNITTING WITH TWO COLOURS

This is just like ordinary knitting, but you work some stitches in one colour and others in a second colour. The most important thing to remember is to carry the colour you are not using loosely across the back of your work. If you pull it too tightly, your knitting will pucker and look misshapen.

Shape ShIFTiNG

To create your zombies, you will need to feel confident about shaping your work using a variety of methods to increase and decrease the number of stitches on your needle. Read on to discover more.

INCREASING M1

The main way to increase the number of stitches on your needle is to make an additional stitch between two stitches. This is written as M1 – or 'make 1' stitch.

1 Use the tip of your right-hand needle to pick up the horizontal loop between the stitch you have just knitted and the following stitch.

2 Transfer the loop onto your left-hand needle by inserting the needle into the front of the loop. Then you can knit into the back of the loop in the normal way.

3 Your new stitch will now be on your right-hand needle.

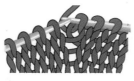

INCREASING INC1

In some cases, you will need to increase the number of stitches slightly differently.

Begin by knitting your stitch in the normal way. Rather than slipping the original stitch off the needle, knit again into the back of the original stitch. Now you can slip the original stitch off the needle.

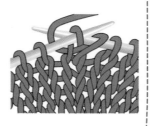

DECREASING K2TOG

This is the simplest way of decreasing and involves putting your needle through two stitches instead of one, then knitting them in the normal way.

DECREASING P2TOG

This is just like knitting two stitches together, only you purl the stitches instead of knitting them.

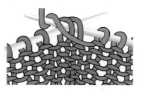

DECREASING SSK

This forms a mirror image to the right-sloping stitch formed by knitting two stitches together. First slip one stitch, then the next stitch, from your left-hand needle to your right-hand needle. Insert the tip of your left-hand needle from left to right through the front of the two slipped stitches, then knit them in the normal way.

DECREASING S1, K2TOG, PSSO

Occasionally you will need to decrease two stitches at a time. For this, first slip one stitch from your left- to your right-hand needle. Then knit two stitches together, as outlined above. Now pass the slipped stitch over the stitch you have just made.

Joining

It can often seem that joining your knitted pieces together takes longer than the knitting itself. But it really is important to take your time over this stage to make sure that you are happy with your finished items.

MATTRESS STITCH

This stitch is used to seam vertical edges, such as the side seams of bodies and garments. A slight variation of the stitch is used to join two horizontal edges such as the lower edges of the zombie bodies.

VERTICAL EDGES

With the two vertical edges together, take your yarn under the running stitch between the first two stitches on one side, then under the running stitch between the first two stitches on the other side. Continue threading your yarn up the seam in this way, pulling the yarn up fairly firmly every few stitches.

HORIZONTAL EDGES

With the two horizontal edges together, take your yarn round the two 'legs' of the outermost row of stitches on one piece of knitting and then under the two corresponding 'legs' of the second piece of knitting. Continue in this way, pulling the yarn up fairly firmly every few stitches.

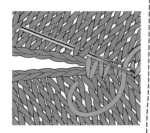

OVERSEWING

This is used for seaming curved edges or sewing very small items together. For most projects, you will use a combination of oversewing and mattress stitch. The stitch is usually worked on the reverse side of your knitting, but is sometimes used on the front.

To oversew a seam, take your yarn from the front over the edges of your seam and back through the front, a little further along.

PICKING UP STITCHES ALONG A HORIZONTAL EDGE

Sometimes you will need to pick up stitches along a horizontal edge of your knitting, in order to knit another part of the project.

With the right side of your work facing you, insert your needle into the first stitch where you want to create a new stitch. Wind the yarn round the tip of your needle and pull the new loop through, just as if you were knitting a normal stitch. Continue until you have the required number of stitches.

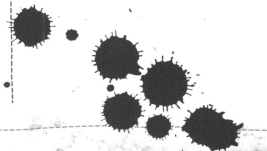

The FiniShing LiNE

To add finishing touches such as blood splats, wounds and gruesome facial features to your knitted items, you will need to know a few basic embroidery stitches and some other useful techniques and handy hints.

FRENCH KNOT

These are used for the centres of some of the eyes and for the blood splats and pimples.

Bring your yarn out at your starting point, within the yarn strand rather than between stitches. Wind the yarn twice around your needle, keeping the yarn fairly taut. Take the point of your needle back down into your knitting, just by your starting point, again within the yarn strand. Take your needle out at the starting point for the next stitch or in an inconspicuous area where you can secure and trim the yarn. Pull your yarn through your work so that the knot slides off the needle and onto your knitting.

CHAIN STITCH

This is used for the eyes, some of the noses, wounds, edging for holes and other markings. You can work chain stitch in rows, curved lines or circles.

Bring your yarn out at the starting point. Take your needle back into the knitting, just by your original starting point, leaving a small loop of yarn. Bring your needle back up through your knitting a stitch width along and catch the yarn loop. Pull your yarn up quite firmly. Repeat this process until the stitching is the required length.

STRAIGHT STITCH

This is used for the stitches worked over the wounds and scars and for a few other decorative touches. Simply take your yarn out at your starting point and back down into your knitting where you want the stitch to end. Bring your needle back out at the point where you want to make the next stitch.

SATIN STITCH

This stitch is used for some of the zombies' mouths. It consists of a series of straight stitches worked very closely together.

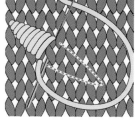

Take your needle out at your starting point. Insert your needle back into your work and out again near the starting point, ready to work the next stitch. Continue in this way until the shape is filled.

USING A SEPARATED STRAND

For some of the embroidery you will need to separate your yarn into two thinner lengths or – in a few cases – into a single strand. Separated strands can be quite delicate. To make sure your yarn doesn't break, always pull on it very gently from close to your work. You should also make sure that the length of yarn you are working with is no longer than you need.

STARTING & FINISHING EMBROIDERY

To begin embroidering on your zombies, tie a double knot in the end of your yarn. Take your needle between stitches at the back of your work (or a nearby inconspicuous area) and out to your starting point. Pull gently on the yarn so that the knot disappears into the inside of your work. When you have finished the embroidery, take your yarn back out to an inconspicuous area. Work a couple of tiny stitches, one over the other, round the running thread between the knitted stitches. (The running threads will be slightly sunken so the stitches will be virtually invisible.) Conceal the remaining yarn tail as outlined under Weaving In Ends (see right).

When you are working embroidery on a flat item such as the zombies' clothes, you can simply tie a knot in your yarn at both the beginning and end of your work, and trim the yarn closely.

CROCHET CHAINS

1 Form a slip knot on your crochet hook, as if you were starting to cast on some knitting. Wind the yarn round your crochet hook from the back to the front, catching the yarn in the slot of the hook.

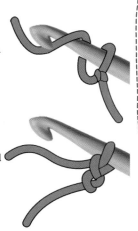

2 Use the hook to pull a loop of yarn through the slip stitch to form the second chain. Continue in this way, pulling each loop up fairly tightly, until your chain is the required length.

SOAK AWAY

Sometimes when you have stitched an item together, the shape is not exactly as you want. In this case, soak the item in lukewarm water, then squeeze out the excess water, reshape the item and leave it to dry.

SEWING ON FASTENINGS

Sew the Velcro tape to your knitting by oversewing round the edges. Remember to take your needle fairly deeply into your work to make sure the tape is secure.

Sew the snap fasteners to your knitting by sewing several times through the four holes on the outside edge of the fasteners. It is helpful to use your thread double when you do this to make it stronger. Take your needle fairly deeply into your work to make sure the fasteners are secure and remember not to pull too tightly or you will risk breaking the thread on the edges of the hole.

SEWING ON BUTTONS & BEADS

Secure the buttons using normal sewing thread. Secure the beads by working a few back stitches through the hole in each bead, again using normal sewing thread.

WEAVING IN ENDS

You can conceal the yarn ends or 'tails' on stuffed items within the item itself. Use your needle to take the yarn end into the item and out again. Squash the item slightly, pull the yarn taut and then trim it close to your knitting. When the item regains its normal shape, the yarn end will be concealed inside.

With items such as the zombies' clothes, weave in the yarn tails by working a few running stitches backwards and forwards along the seam allowance. It helps to work the running stitches within the yarn strands to help them stay put.

ReanimATing YOUR ZOMbIES

All the zombies in this book are constructed using the same general sewing techniques. The Velcro and snap fasteners allow you to rip them up with ease!

THE HEAD

Place the two head pieces right sides together and oversew round the sides and lower edge of the head. Turn the piece right side out. Stuff and then close the top of the head, using mattress stitch. Sew the loop part of the Velcro fastening to the centre back of the head. The fastening should be vertical and the lower edge should be about 1.5 cm (¾ in) up from the bottom of the head.

THE UPPER BODY

Form the front upper body piece into a box shape, so that the right side of your knitting is on the inside of the 'box'. Oversew the short seams at the corners. Turn the 'box' right side out. Join the back upper body piece to the front using mattress stitch, leaving the lower edge open for stuffing. Stuff the piece and close the lower edge, using mattress stitch.

THE LOWER BODY & LEGS

Join the front and back of the lower body in the same way as the upper body.

Attach the hook part of the Velcro fastening to the top of the lower body and the loop part to the lower part of the upper body.

Fold the leg pieces in half lengthways so that the right sides are together. Oversew the lower, back and top seams of the foot. Turn the piece right side out and use mattress stitch to sew the back leg seams. Stuff the legs and oversew them to the base of the lower body.

ARMS

Fold the arm pieces in half lengthways, so that the right side of your knitting is on the inside. Oversew round the hand. Turn the piece right side out and use mattress stitch to sew the arm seams. Stuff lightly. Fold the top flap of the arm down across the opening to form a flat surface and oversew the edges in place. Stitch the stud side of the snap fasteners to the flat top section of each arm. Stitch the socket side of the snap fasteners to the top sides of the upper body.

Classic ZOMBIE

People (that's you, dear reader) are used to zombies. They've featured in our movies for decades now, in all kinds of forms, from the silent, rather dignified early option – check out *I Walked With a Zombie* (1943) – to the much more aggressive creations of George Romero or Quentin Tarantino. To start you off on your knitting journey, we're opening with Classic Zombie. Dishevelled and damaged, yet disconcertingly lively, his vibe is energetic, even upbeat – this is one zombie who's ready to rumble.

THEY WON'T STAY DEAD!

An IMAGE TEN Production

NIGHT OF THE LIVING DEAD

They keep coming back in a bloodthirsty lust for HUMAN FLESH!...

Pits the dead against the living in a struggle for survival!

Starring JUDITH O'DEA · DUANE JONES · MARILYN EASTMAN · KARL HARDMAN · JUDITH RIDLEY · KEITH WAYNE
Produced by Russel W. Streiner and Karl Hardman · Directed by George A. Romero · Screenplay by John A. Russo · A Walter Reade Organization Presentation – Released by Continental

PEDIGREE

1929 *The Magic Island*, the first novel introducing the word 'zombi' to popular culture, is published.

1936 Boris Karloff stars in *The Walking Dead*; over 70 years later, a smash-hit US TV series of the same name prompted a fresh zombie craze.

1968 The introduction of recognizable zombies in the modern style, with the release of George Romero's *Night of the Living Dead* (left).

Classic ZOMBIE

With his dangling eye and gaping mouth, this apparition is every inch the classic zombie. Dressed in dowdy, tattered clothes and with the last word in bad hair days, this poor fellow has wounds all over the place, and his guts are spilling out of his middle in vile woolly festoons. Don't worry too much, though – they tuck neatly into their own specially made pouch should you prefer it that way.

YOU WILL NEED

70 m/77 yd (28 g/1 oz) beige DK yarn

Small amounts of dark red, cream and dark grey DK yarns

15 m/16½ yd (6 g/¼ oz) bright red DK yarn

Very small amounts of purple and black DK yarns

Small amount of yellow mohair or mohair/silk yarn

31 m/34 yd (8 g/¼ oz) rust 4-ply yarn

26 m/28½ yd (6.5 g/¼ oz) variegated grey 4-ply yarn

30 g/1 oz polyester toy filling

Cream sewing thread

Twelve medium dark green bugle beads

Three small white bugle beads

A glass bead for the eye

A piece of Velcro tape in white, measuring 2.5 x 1 cm (1 x ⅜ in)

A piece of Velcro tape in white, measuring 5 x 2 cm (2 x ¾ in)

Two 13-mm (½-in) snap fasteners

YOU WILL ALSO NEED

A pair of 3 mm (US 2/3) knitting needles

A yarn needle to sew your items together

An embroidery needle

An ordinary sewing needle

A grey crayon

THE DOLL
HEAD
MAKE 2 PIECES
- Cast on 10 sts in beige.
- Work 6 rows in st st, beg with a K row.
- Next row: [K1, M1] twice, K6, [M1, K1] twice. (14 sts)
- Next row: P.
- Next row: K2, M1, K to last 2 sts, M1, K2. (16 sts)
- Next row: P.
- Rep last 2 rows once more. (18 sts)
- Work 12 rows in st st, beg with a K row.
- Next row: K2, [k2tog] twice, K6, [ssk] twice, K2. (14 sts)
- Next row: P2tog, P10, p2tog. (12 sts)
- Cast off.

UPPER BODY
The upper body is knitted from the top to the bottom.
FRONT
MAKE 1
- Cast on 14 sts in beige.
- Work 6 rows in st st, beg with a K row.
- Next row: Cast on 4 sts, K to end. (18 sts)
- Next row: Cast on 4 sts, P to end. (22 sts)
- Work 10 rows in st st, beg with a K row.
- Next row: K8, P3, turn and work on these 11 sts only, leaving rem 11 sts on needle.
- Next row: K3, P8.
- Next row: K8, P3.
- Rep last 2 rows 4 times more.
- Break yarn and join it to rem 11 sts on RS of work.
- Next row: P3, K8.
- Next row: P8, K3.
- Rep last 2 rows 4 times more.
- Next row: P3, K8.

- Now work across all 22 sts.
- Work 2 rows in st st, beg with a P row.
- Next row: P4, K14, P4.
- Next row: Cast off 4 sts, K to last 4 sts, cast off 4 sts. (14 sts)
- Break yarn and rejoin it to WS of work.
- Work 5 rows in st st, beg with a P row.
- Cast off.

BACK
MAKE 1
- Cast on 14 sts in beige.
- Work 24 rows in st st, beg with a K row.
- Cast off.

GUT POCKET
MAKE 1
- Cast on 8 sts in beige.
- 1st row: Inc1, K to last 2 sts, inc1, K1. (10 sts)
- Next row: P.
- Rep last 2 rows once more. (12 sts)
- Work 10 rows in st st, beg with a K row.
- Next row: K1, k2tog, K to last 3 sts, ssk, K1. (10 sts)
- Next row: P.
- Rep last 2 rows once more. (8 sts)
- Cast off.

GUTS
STOMACH
MAKE 1
- Cast on 5 sts in dark red.
- 1st row: Inc1, K2, inc1, K1. (7 sts)
- Next row: P.
- Next row: K1, M1, K to last st, M1, K1. (9 sts)
- Next row: P.
- Rep last 2 rows once more. (11 sts)

- Work 4 rows in st st, beg with a K row.
- Next row: K1, k2tog, K to last 3 sts, ssk, K1. (9 sts)
- Next row: P.
- Rep last 2 rows once more. (7 sts)
- Next row: K1, k2tog, K1, ssk, K1. (5 sts)
- Cast off kwise.

INTESTINES
MAKE 1
- Cast on 40 sts in dark red.
- 1st row: K.
- Cast off.

LOWER BODY
FRONT
MAKE 1

- Cast on 14 sts in beige.
- Work 6 rows in st st, beg with a K row.
- Next row: Cast on 4 sts, K to end. (18 sts)
- Next row: Cast on 4 sts, P to end. (22 sts)
- Work 7 rows in st st, beg with a K row.
- Next row: P4, K14, P4.
- Next row: Cast off 4 sts, K to last 4 sts, cast off 4 sts. (14 sts)
- Break yarn and rejoin it to WS of work.
- Work 5 rows in st st, beg with a P row.
- Cast off.

BACK
MAKE 1

- Cast on 14 sts in beige.
- Work 8 rows in st st, beg with a K row.
- Cast off.

FIRST LEG
MAKE 1

- Cast on 30 sts in beige.
- Work 6 rows in st st, beg with a K row.
- Next row: K6, cast off 18 sts, K to end. (12 sts) *
- Work 23 rows in st st, beg with a P row.
- Cast off.

SECOND LEG
OUTER LEG
MAKE 1

- Work as for first leg until *.
- Work 5 rows in st st, beg with a P row.
- Next row: K5, P2, turn and work on these 7 sts only, leaving rem 5 sts on needle.
- Next row: K2, P5.
- Next row: K5, P2.
- Rep last 2 rows 5 times more.
- Break yarn and rejoin it to rem 5 sts on RS of work.
- Next row: P2, K3.
- Next row: P3, K2.
- Next row: P2, K3.
- Rep last 2 rows 5 times more.
- Now work across all 12 sts.
- Work 5 rows in st st, beg with a P row.
- Cast off.

INNER LEG
MAKE 1

- Cast on 26 sts in bright red.
- Work 4 rows in st st, beg with a K row.
- Next row: K5, cast off 16 sts, K to end. (10 sts)
- Work 21 rows in st st, beg with a P row.
- Cast off.

FIRST ARM
MAKE 1

- Cast on 4 sts in beige.
- Work 4 rows in st st, beg with a K row.
- Next row: Cast on 3 sts, K to end. (7 sts)
- Next row: Cast on 3 sts, P to end. (10 sts) *
- Work 30 rows in st st, beg with a K row.
- Next row: K1, k2tog, K4, ssk, K1. (8 sts)
- Next row: P2tog, P4, p2tog. (6 sts)
- Break yarn, thread it through rem sts and secure.

SECOND ARM
OUTER ARM
MAKE 1

- Work as for first arm until *.
- Work 20 rows in st st, beg with a K row.
- Break yarn and thread it through rem sts but do not pull up tightly or secure.

INNER ARM
MAKE 1

- Cast on 8 sts in bright red.
- Work 28 rows in st st, beg with a K row.

- Next row: K1, k2tog, K2, ssk, K1. (6 sts)
- Next row: P2tog, P2, p2tog. (4 sts)
- Break yarn, thread it through rem sts and secure.

MAKING UP & DECORATING

To make the split on the elbow of the second arm, embroider a ring of small, tight chain stitches in beige and snip the threads within the circle to create a hole.

Sew the head, body, arms and legs together, as outlined in the instructions on page 17. Remember to leave the second leg and the second arm (the pieces with 'splits') unstuffed.

Fold the gut pocket in half widthways, with right sides facing inwards, and oversew the sides together. Oversew the top edges of the pocket just below the outer edges of the gap on the upper body, so that the seams of the pocket are at the top and bottom of the gap and the right side of the knitting is on the inside of the pocket.

Fold the stomach piece in half with the right side on the outside to form a semi-circle. Oversew the curved seam, stuffing the piece lightly as you go. Oversew the long seam of the intestine piece and attach it to one corner of the stomach.

Join the inner leg in the same way as the other leg pieces and stuff lightly. Insert the inner leg into the main unstuffed leg. Secure the split on the outer leg

to the inner leg. Work a row of chain stitch on the inner part of the leg in purple. Work a few straight stitches in beige over the edge, as shown in the photograph.

Sew the inner arm piece together in a similar way to the other arm pieces and stuff lightly. Insert the inner arm into the main unstuffed arm. Carefully pull out the yarn threaded through the final row of stitches and oversew the edge to the inner arm. Finish the top of the arm as for the first arm. Complete the top of the arm as outlined in the general instructions.

Using cream yarn, embroider the ribs in chain stitch, using the photograph as a guide.

Sew the green bugle beads to the hands and feet to represent the nails.

Using dark grey yarn, embroider a ring of chain stitch for the eye socket. Using the same yarn, embroider the nose in satin stitch, working a straight stitch down the sides to neaten the edges. Using black yarn, embroider the mouth in satin stitch, using vertical stitches. Work around the mouth in chain stitch. Using a separated strand of bright red yarn, embroider the blood trickling from the mouth in chain stitch. Sew three small white bugle beads onto the mouth to represent the teeth. Using dark red yarn, join the eye bead to the head, using a single long straight stitch.

Shade the eye socket, using the grey crayon.

For the hair, cut 16 lengths, each 20 cm (8 in) long, of yellow mohair yarn and divide them into two bunches of eight lengths. Join the centre of the bunches to each side of the head.

JACKET
LEFT SIDE
MAKE 1
- Cast on 14 sts in rust 4-ply.
- 1st row: K.
- Next row: K3, P11.
- Rep last 2 rows 10 times more.
- Next row: K2, M1, K to end. (15 sts)
- Next row: K3, P to end.
- Next row: K.
- Next row: K3, P to end.
- Rep last 4 rows once more. (16 sts)
- Next row: K6, P5, K5.
- Next row: K3, P2, K5, P6.
- Next row: K6, P1, K3, P1, K5.
- Next row: K3, P2, K1, P3, K1, P6.
- Rep last 2 rows once more.
- Next row: K.
- Next row: K3, P13.
- Rep last 2 rows 3 times more.
- K 5 rows.
- Cast off.

RIGHT SIDE
MAKE 1
- Cast on 14 sts in rust 4-ply.
- 1st row: K.
- Next row: P11, K3.
- Rep last 2 rows 10 times more.
- Next row: K to last 2 sts, M1, K2. (15 sts)
- Next row: P to last 3 sts, K3.
- Next row: K.
- Next row: P to last 3 sts, K3.

- Rep last 4 rows once more. (16 sts)
- Next row: K5, P5, K6.
- Next row: P6, K5, P2, K3.
- Next row: K5, P1, K3, P1, K6.
- Next row: P6, K1, P3, K1, P2, K3.
- Rep last 2 rows once more.
- Next row: K.
- Next row: P13, K3.
- Rep last 2 rows 3 times more.
- K 5 rows.
- Cast off.

BACK
MAKE 1
- Cast on 22 sts in rust 4-ply.
- Work 22 rows in st st, beg with a K row.
- Next row: K2, M1, K to last 2 sts, M1, K2. (24 sts)
- Work 3 rows in st st, beg with a P row.
- Rep last 4 rows once more. (26 sts)
- Work 14 rows in st st, beg with a K row.
- K 5 rows.
- Cast off.

LEFT SLEEVE
MAKE 1
- Cast on 14 sts in rust 4-ply.
- Work 24 rows in st st, beg with a P row.
- Cast off.

RIGHT SLEEVE
MAKE 1
- Cast on 14 sts in rust 4-ply.
- Work 31 rows in st st, beg with a P row.
- Cast off.

MAKING UP
Sew the long seams of the sleeves, using mattress stitch. With the two side and back pieces right sides outwards, oversew 15 mm (⁵⁄₈ in) along each side of the top edges to form the shoulder seams. Join the sides using running stitch, leaving the top 3 cm (1¼ in) open to form the armholes. Insert the sleeves into the armholes of the main piece and oversew around the armholes from the inside. For the holes, work a flattened circle of chain stitch in rust 4-ply where you want the holes to be, then cut your knitting on the inside of the shape.

TROUSERS
MAKE 1
- Cast on 20 sts in variegated grey 4-ply yarn for first leg.
- Work 16 rows in st st, beg with a K row.
- Break yarn and leave sts on needle.
- Cast on 20 sts for second leg.

- Work 16 rows in st st, beg with a K row.
- Next row: K 20 sts from second leg then 20 sts from first leg. (40 sts)
- Work 17 rows in st st, beg with a P row.
- Next row: [K2, P2] to end.
- Rep last row 3 times more.
- Cast off, keeping to the K2, P2 pattern.

MAKING UP
Using mattress stitch, join the back seam of the trousers so that the lowest part of the seam is level with the crotch. Then join the two inside leg seams, again using mattress stitch. Using matching yarn, work a border of chain stitch about 1 cm (³⁄₈ in) up from the lower edge of one leg. Trim off the knitting below this to form a frayed edging. Work the holes in the same way as described for the jacket, left.

Rat

THE DOLL
BODY & HEAD
FIRST SIDE
MAKE 1

- Cast on 18 sts in dark brown.
- 1st row: K to last 3 sts, ssk, K1. (17 sts)
- Next row: P2tog, P to end. (16 sts)
- Next row: K1, k2tog, K to last 3 sts, ssk, K1. (14 sts)
- Next row: P2tog, P to end. (13 sts)
- Rep last 4 rows once more. (8 sts)
- Cast off.

SECOND SIDE
MAKE 1

- Cast on 18 sts in dark brown.
- 1st row: K1, k2tog, K to end. (17 sts)
- Next row: P to last 2 sts, p2tog. (16 sts)
- Next row: K1, k2tog, K to last 3 sts, ssk, K1. (14 sts)
- Next row: P to last 2 sts, p2tog. (13 sts)
- Rep last 4 rows once more. (8 sts)
- Cast off.

EARS
MAKE 1

- Using the crochet hook, make a 4-chain crochet chain in dark brown.

TAIL
MAKE 1

- Using the crochet hook, make a 7-cm (2¾-in) crochet chain in dark brown.

MAKING UP

Place the two body and head pieces right sides together and oversew the edges, leaving a gap at the lower edge for turning and stuffing. Turn the rat the right way out, stuff and close the gap.

With black yarn, embroider two French knots for the eyes. Using a separated strand of white yarn, work a ring of chain stitch around each French knot. Using black yarn, work a French knot for the nose. Add the whiskers, using cream thread.

Form the ear chains into small loops and fasten to the head, using the yarn 'tails'.

Thread one yarn tail up through the tail and use the yarn tails to join the tail to the end of the body.

Frankenstein's MONSTER

Y ou probably know (as any self-respecting horror fan should) that Frankenstein isn't the name of the monster, but that of his creator. Stitched and patched together, this woolly frightener follows the prescription from the cult 1931 movie: squared-off head, vacant glare and horrid green pallor. He's finished off with a bolt through his neck – this is a man-made monster, after all. Poignantly, he's rather smartly dressed – in a classic dark suit, a shade too small. Really, he'd just like to fit in with the crowd.

PEDIGREE

1818 *Frankenstein* the novel is conceived by Mary Shelley as the result of one of those after-dinner games that everyone regrets in the morning.

1910 The first Frankenstein-themed moving picture is made in the Bronx in New York (featuring a rather unconvincing monster).

1931 The movie *Frankenstein* (right), James Whales' classic and the model for all its successors, appears in cinemas. And the rest is history . . .

UNIVERSAL PRESENTA
FRANKENSTEIN
CON
COLIN CLIVE
MAE CLARKE
JOHN BOLES
BORIS KARLOFF
BASADA EN LA HISTORIA de MARY WOLLSTONE CROFT SHELLEY
DIRIGIDA POR JAMES WHALE

Frankenstein's MONSTER

Huge, ugly and patched together from odd body parts, Frankenstein's monster has been driven by sorrow and loneliness to commit the most terrible crimes. But though he's not a pretty face, the monster has a kinder side to him; most of all, he wants to meet someone who will accept him for himself. Knit your own version and show him that at least you love him for who he is.

YOU WILL NEED

70 m/77 yd (28 g/1 oz) green DK yarn

43 m/47 yd (17 g/⅝ oz) black DK yarn

Small amounts of white and red DK yarns

27 m/30 yd (11 g/⅜ oz) dark brown DK yarn

30 g/1 oz polyester toy filling

Cream sewing thread

A 40-mm (1½-in) nut and bolt

A 13-mm (½-in) dark brown button

A 13-mm (½-in) dark red button

A piece of Velcro tape in beige, measuring 2.5 x 1 cm (1 x ⅜ in)

A piece of Velcro tape in beige, measuring 5 x 2 cm (2 x ¾ in)

Two 13-mm (½-in) snap fasteners

YOU WILL ALSO NEED

A pair of 3 mm (US 2/3) knitting needles

A pair of 2.75 mm (US 2) knitting needles

A yarn needle to sew your items together

An embroidery needle

An ordinary sewing needle

A grey crayon

THE DOLL
HEAD
FRONT
MAKE 1

- Using 3 mm (US 2/3) needles, cast on 10 sts in green.
- 1st row: Inc1, K7, inc1, K1. (12 sts)
- Work 3 rows in st st, beg with a P row.
- Next row: K2, M1, K to last 2 sts, M1, K2. (14 sts)
- Next row: P.
- Rep last 2 rows twice more. (18 sts)
- * Work 15 rows in st st, beg with a K row.
- Next row: P2tog, P14, p2tog. (16 sts)
- Cast off.

BACK
MAKE 1

- Using 3 mm (US 2/3) needles, cast on 10 sts in green.
- 1st row: Inc1, K7, inc1, K1. (12 sts)
- Work 3 rows in st st, beg with a P row.
- Next row: K2, M1, K1, yf, k2tog, K3, yf, k2tog, M1, K2. (14 sts)
- Next row: P.
- Next row: K2, M1, K to last 2 sts, M1, K2. (16 sts)
- Next row: P.
- Rep last 2 rows once more. (18 sts)
- Cont as for front from * to end.

EARS
MAKE 2

- Using 2.75 mm (US 2) needles, cast on 8 sts in green.
- 1st row: K2tog, K4, ssk. (6 sts)
- Next row: P2tog, P2, p2tog. (4 sts)
- Next row: K2tog, ssk. (2 sts)

- Next row: P2tog.
- Break yarn and pull it through rem st.

UPPER BODY

The upper body is knitted from the top to the bottom.

FRONT
MAKE 1

- Using 3 mm (US 2/3) needles, cast on 20 sts in green.
- Work 6 rows in st st, beg with a K row.
- Next row: Cast on 4 sts, K to end. (24 sts)
- Next row: Cast on 4 sts, P to end. (28 sts)
- Work 6 rows in st st, beg with a K row.
- Next row: K4, k2tog, K to last 6 sts, ssk, K4. (26 sts)
- Work 5 rows in st st, beg with a P row.
- Rep last 6 rows twice more. (22 sts)
- Next row: K.
- Next row: P4, K14, P4.
- Next row: Cast off 4 sts, K to last 4 sts, cast off 4 sts. (14 sts)
- Break yarn and rejoin it to WS of work.
- Work 5 rows in st st, beg with a P row.
- Cast off.

BACK
MAKE 1

- Using 3 mm (US 2/3) needles, cast on 20 sts in green.
- Work 6 rows in st st, beg with a K row.
- Next row: K2, k2tog, K to last 4 sts, ssk, K2. (18 sts)
- Work 5 rows in st st, beg with a P row.
- Rep last 6 rows twice more. (14 sts)
- Cast off.

LOWER BODY
FRONT
MAKE 1

- Using 3 mm (US 2/3) needles, cast on 14 sts in green.
- Work 6 rows in st st, beg with a K row.
- Next row: Cast on 4 sts, K to end. (18 sts)
- Next row: Cast on 4 sts, P to end. (22 sts)
- Work 7 rows in st st, beg with a K row.
- Next row: P4, K14, P4.
- Next row: Cast off 4 sts, K to last 4 sts, cast off 4 sts. (14 sts)
- Break yarn and rejoin it to WS of work.
- Work 5 rows in st st, beg with a P row.
- Cast off.

BACK
MAKE 1

- Using 3 mm (US 2/3) needles, cast on 14 sts in green.
- Work 8 rows in st st, beg with a K row.
- Cast off.

LEGS
MAKE 2
- Using 3 mm (US 2/3) needles, cast on 30 sts in green.
- Work 6 rows in st st, beg with a K row.
- Next row: K6, cast off 18 sts,
- K to end. (12 sts)
- Work 19 rows in st st, beg with a P row.
- Cast off.

ARMS
MAKE 2
- Using 3 mm (US 2/3) needles, cast on 4 sts in green.
- Work 4 rows in st st, beg with a K row.
- Next row: Cast on 3 sts, K to end. (7 sts)
- Next row: Cast on 3 sts, P to end. (10 sts)
- Work 28 rows in st st, beg with a K row.
- Next row: K2, M1, K3, M1, K3, M1, K2. (13 sts)
- Work 3 rows in st st, beg with a P row.
- Next row: K2, k2tog, K5, ssk, K2. (11 sts)
- Next row: P2tog, P7, p2tog. (9 sts)
- Cast off.

MAKING UP & DECORATING
Sew the head, body, leg and arm pieces together, as outlined in the instructions on page 17.

Oversew the ears to the sides of the head.

Using black yarn, work two French knots for the eyes. Work a semi-circle of chain stitch around the lower half of each French knot, using white yarn. Work a straight stitch for the mouth, using a separated strand of red yarn. Using another separated strand of red yarn, work the scar in chain stitch. Work a series of straight stitches over the scar, using a separated strand of green yarn. Work the brows, nose and inner cheeks in chain stitch, using green yarn. Work a series of straight stitches for the hair, using black yarn.

Using the grey crayon, add shadows beneath the eyes.

Put the bolt through the back of the head at the side of the 'neck' and secure it with the nut at the other side.

JACKET
The two front sides and the back of the jacket are knitted as one piece, from the lower edge to the neck edge.
MAKE 1
- Using 3 mm (US 2/3) needles, cast on 48 sts in black.
- K 2 rows.
- Next row: K2, P to last 2 sts, K2.
- Next row: K.
- Rep last 2 rows 9 times more.
- Next row: K2, P to last 2 sts, K2.
- Next row: K14, turn and work on these sts only, leaving rem sts on needle.
- Next row: P12, K2.
- Next row: K.
- Rep last 2 rows twice more.
- Next row: P12, K2.
- Next row: Cast off 3 sts, K to end. (11 sts)
- Break yarn and leave sts on needle.
- Rejoin yarn to rem 34 sts on needle on RS of work.
- Next row: K20, turn and work on these sts only, leaving rem sts on needle.
- Work 8 rows in st st, beg with a P row.
- Break yarn and leave sts on needle.
- Rejoin yarn to rem 14 sts on needle on RS of work.
- Next row: K.
- Next row: K2, P12.
- Rep last 2 rows 3 times more.
- Next row: Cast off 3 sts, K to end then K across the other 31 sts on needle. (42 sts)
- Next row: K11, [k2tog] 4 times, K4, [ssk] 4 times, K11. (34 sts)
- K 3 rows.
- Cast off.

SLEEVES
MAKE 2
- Using 3 mm (US 2/3) needles, cast on 14 sts in black.
- Work 24 rows in st st, beg with a K row.
- Cast off.

MAKING UP
With the right sides of the jacket together, oversew the shoulder seams. Join the sleeve seams, using mattress stitch. Insert each sleeve into an armhole of the main piece and oversew them from the inside. Overlap the left border over the right border of the jacket and sew on one of the buttons. Sew the other button above this on the right border.

TROUSERS
MAKE 1
- Using 3 mm (US 2/3) needles, cast on 20 sts in dark brown for first leg.
- Work 12 rows in st st, beg with a K row.
- Next row: K3, cast off 3 sts, K to end. (17 sts)
- Next row: P14, turn and cast on 3 sts, turn again and P to end. (20 sts)
- Work 4 rows in st st, beg with a K row.
- Break yarn and leave sts on needle.
- Cast on 20 sts for second leg.
- Work 8 rows in st st, beg with a K row.
- Next row: K12, cast off 3 sts, K to end. (17 sts)
- Next row: P5, turn and cast on 3 sts, turn again and P to end. (20 sts)
- Work 8 rows in st st, beg with a K row.

- Next row: K 20 sts from second leg, then 20 sts from first leg. (40 sts)
- Work 9 rows in st st, beg with a P row.
- Next row: K29, cast off 3 sts, K to end. (37 sts)
- Next row: P8, turn and cast on 3 sts, turn again and P to end. (40 sts)
- Work 4 rows in st st, beg with a K row.

- Next row: [K2, P2] to end.
- Rep last row 3 times more.
- Cast off, keeping to the K2, P2 pattern.

MAKING UP
Using mattress stitch, join the back seam of the trousers so that the lowest part of the seam is level with the crotch. Then join the two inside leg seams, again using mattress stitch.

Zombie COP

This isn't the friendly, doughnut-loving lunk you're familiar with from untold numbers of cop shows – this bloated little monster has a taste for altogether less wholesome fare. Wielding a truncheon fashioned from a thigh bone, wearing a rotten old uniform covered in gore and with fuzzy features in quite an advanced state of puffy decay, there are plenty of clues to tell you that Zombie Cop's law-enforcement days are long over. It's not only the bad guys who'll be running just as fast as they can.

PEDiGREE

1995 *In The Mouth of Madness* (left), directed by John Carpenter, features some seriously scary zombie cop action.

1996 The game 'Resident Evil' is released, spawning a franchise covering everything from movies to soft toys. Its lurching zombie policemen are among the most frightening of the genre.

2010 *The Walking Dead* is adapted from black-and-white comic book to TV series. It features undead cops, but its complex police hero, Rick Grimes, hasn't turned zombie . . . yet.

Zombie COP

Spotty, goofy, decomposed . . . you name it.
This law enforcer is hardly a looker, even by
zombie standards – that bruised, swollen eye
is the icing on the cake. There are plenty of
reminders of his day job, though, including
some effective little handcuffs and a fine,
peaked uniform hat.

YOU WILL NEED

70 m/77 yd (28 g/1 oz) pale brown
DK yarn

Very small amounts of red and
green DK yarns

Small amounts of black and cream
DK yarns

Very small amount of black mohair
or mohair/silk yarn

33 m/36 yd (13 g/½ oz) pale blue
DK yarn

27 m/30 yd (12 g/½ oz) royal blue
DK yarn

14 m/15½ yd (6 g/¼ oz) mid-blue
DK yarn

30 g/1 oz polyester toy filling

Cream sewing thread

Three small white glass bugle
beads

Two small dark grey buttons

A small metal star brad

A small metal button

Two 17-mm (¾-in) metal toggle
rings joined with a short length of
chain for the handcuffs

A 6-cm (2½-in) length of plastic
drinking straw

A piece of Velcro tape in beige,
measuring 2.5 x 1 cm (1 x ⅜ in)

A piece of Velcro tape in beige,
measuring 5 x 2 cm (2 x ¾ in)

Two 13-mm (½-in) snap fasteners

YOU WILL ALSO NEED

A pair of 3 mm (US 2/3) knitting
needles

A yarn needle to sew your items
together

An embroidery needle

An ordinary sewing needle

A grey crayon

THE DOLL
HEAD
BACK
MAKE 1

- Cast on 18 sts in pale brown.
- 1st row: Inc1, K to last 2 sts, inc1, K1. (20 sts)
- Work 7 rows in st st, beg with a P row. *
- Next row: K2, k2tog, K to last 4 sts, ssk, K2. (18 sts)
- Next row: P.
- Rep last 2 rows twice more. (14 sts)
- Work 6 rows in st st, beg with a K row.
- Next row: K2, [k2tog] twice, K2, [ssk] twice, K2. (10 sts)
- Next row: P2tog, P to last 2 sts, p2tog. (8 sts)
- Cast off.

FRONT
MAKE 1

- Work as for back until *.
- Next row: K2, k2tog, K5, [K1, P1, K1] into next 2 sts, turn and P6 sts, turn again and K6 sts, turn again and P6 sts, turn again and k2tog, K2, ssk, K5, ssk, K2. (20 sts)
- Next row: P.
- Next row: K2, k2tog, K4, k2tog, ssk, K4, ssk, K2. (16 sts)
- Next row: P.
- Next row: K2, k2tog, K to last 4 sts, ssk, K2. (14 sts)
- Work 7 rows in st st, beg with a P row.
- Next row: K2, [k2tog] twice, K2, [ssk] twice, K2. (10 sts)
- Next row: P2tog, P to last 2 sts, p2tog. (8 sts)
- Cast off.

EAR
MAKE 1

- Cast on 5 sts in pale brown.
- 1st row: K.
- Next row: P2tog, K1, p2tog. (3 sts)
- Next row: S1, k2tog, psso.
- Break yarn and pull it through rem st.

UPPER BODY
The upper body is knitted from the top to the bottom.

FRONT
MAKE 1

- Cast on 20 sts in pale brown.
- Work 6 rows in st st, beg with a K row.
- Next row: Cast on 4 sts, K to end. (24 sts)
- Next row: Cast on 4 sts, P to end. (28 sts)
- Work 4 rows in st st, beg with a K row.
- Next row: K4, k2tog, K to last 6 sts, ssk, K4. (26 sts)
- Work 5 rows in st st, beg with a P row.
- Rep last 6 rows twice more. (22 sts)
- Next row: K.
- Next row: P4, K14, P4.
- Next row: Cast off 4 sts, K to last 4 sts, cast off 4 sts. (14 sts)
- Break yarn and rejoin it to WS of work.
- Work 5 rows in st st, beg with a P row.
- Cast off.

BACK
MAKE 1

- Cast on 20 sts in pale brown.
- Work 4 rows in st st, beg with a K row.
- Next row: K2, k2tog, K to last 4 sts, ssk, K2. (18 sts)
- Work 5 rows in st st, beg with a P row.

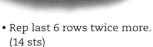

- Rep last 6 rows twice more. (14 sts)
- Work 2 rows in st st, beg with a K row.
- Cast off.

LOWER BODY
FRONT
MAKE 1

- Cast on 14 sts in pale brown.
- Work 6 rows in st st, beg with a K row.
- Next row: Cast on 4 sts, K to end. (18 sts)
- Next row: Cast on 4 sts, P to end. (22 sts)
- Work 7 rows in st st, beg with a K row.
- Next row: P4, K14, P4.
- Next row: Cast off 4 sts, K to last 4 sts, cast off 4 sts. (14 sts)
- Break yarn and rejoin it to WS of work.
- Work 5 rows in st st, beg with a P row.
- Cast off.

BACK
MAKE 1

- Cast on 14 sts in pale brown.
- Work 8 rows in st st.
- Cast off.

LEGS
MAKE 2
- Cast on 28 sts in pale brown.
- Work 6 rows in st st, beg with a K row.
- Next row: K6, cast off 16 sts, K to end. (12 sts)
- Work 21 rows in st st, beg with a P row.
- Cast off.

ARMS
MAKE 2
- Cast on 4 sts in pale brown.
- Work 4 rows in st st, beg with a K row.
- Next row: Cast on 3 sts, K to end. (7 sts)
- Next row: Cast on 3 sts, P to end. (10 sts)
- Work 24 rows in st st, beg with a K row.
- Next row: K2, M1, K3, M1, K3, M1, K2. (13 sts)
- Work 3 rows in st st, beg with a P row.
- Next row: K2, k2tog, K to last 4 sts, ssk, K2. (11 sts)
- Next row: P2tog, P to last 2 sts, p2tog. (9 sts)
- Cast off.

MAKING UP & DECORATING
Sew the head, body, arms and legs together as outlined in the instructions on page 17.

Using red yarn, work a few rows of chain stitch on one arm for the wound. Work a row of chain stitch around the wound, using a separated strand of green yarn.

Stitch the ear in place.

Work a French knot for one of the eyes, using black yarn. Using green yarn, work a ring of chain stitch around the French knot. Using pale brown yarn, work two short rows of chain stitch for the bruised eye. Work a straight stitch across the middle of the two rows, using a separated strand of red yarn. Work a group of seven French knots in pale brown yarn on one cheek. On the other cheek, work three straight stitches, using a separated strand of red yarn. Work a few straight stitches over one of these, using a separated strand of black yarn. Work the outline of the mouth in chain stitch, using black yarn. Work the centre of the mouth in satin stitch, keeping your stitches vertical. Work around one side of the mouth in chain stitch, using a separated strand of red yarn. Sew the three white bugle beads in place for the teeth.

Shade the bruised eye socket, using the grey crayon.

For the hair, cut ten lengths of black mohair yarn, each 7 cm (2¾ in) long. Divide the yarn into two bunches of five lengths and secure at the centres to each side of the head.

SHIRT
MAKE 1
- Cast on 42 sts in pale blue.
- K 2 rows.
- Next row: K2, P to last 2 sts, K2.
- Next row: K.
- Rep last 2 rows 5 times more.
- Next row: K2, P to last 2 sts, K2.
- Next row: K11, turn and work on these 11 sts only, leaving rem sts on needle.
- Next row: P to last 2 sts, K2.
- Next row: K.
- Rep last 2 rows 5 times more.
- Break yarn and leave sts on needle.
- Rejoin yarn to rem sts on RS of work.
- Next row: K20, turn and work on these 20 sts only, leaving 11 rem sts on needle.
- Work 12 rows in st st, beg with a P row.

- Break yarn and leave sts on needle.
- Rejoin yarn to rem sts on RS of work.
- Next row: K.
- Next row: K2, P to end.
- Rep last 2 rows 5 times more.
- Next row: K.
- Now work across all 42 sts.
- Next row: Cast off 3 sts, K to end. (39 sts)
- Rep last row once more. (36 sts)
- K 4 rows.
- Cast off.

FIRST SLEEVE
MAKE 1
- Cast on 18 sts in pale blue.
- 1st row: K.
- Work 12 rows in st st, beg with a K row.
- Cast off.

SECOND SLEEVE
MAKE 1
- Cast on 18 sts in pale blue.
- Work 10 rows in st st, beg with a K row.
- Cast off.

MAKING UP
On the second sleeve, work a row of chain stitch across the sleeve a few rows up from the cast-off edge. Trim your knitting beneath this stitching and unravel the yarn a bit so that it looks loopy. With the right sides of the shirt facing outwards, oversew the front to the back at the shoulders. Join the sleeve seams, using mattress stitch. Insert the sleeves into the armholes of the main piece and oversew them from the inside. Overlap the left border over the right border of the shirt and sew on one of the small buttons. Sew the other button below this on the right border. Fasten the metal brad in place on the chest of the shirt. Using red yarn, work a combination of French knots, some with straight stitches coming out in a star pattern, to represent splattered blood.

TROUSERS
MAKE 1
- Cast on 20 sts in royal blue for first leg.
- 1st row: K.

- Work 20 rows in st st, beg with a K row.
- Break yarn and leave sts on needle.
- Cast on 20 sts for second leg.
- 1st row: K.
- Work 16 rows in st st, beg with a K row.
- Next row: K 20 sts from second leg, then 20 sts from first leg. (40 sts)
- Work 15 rows in st st, beg with a P row.
- Next row: K2, P2 to end.
- Rep last row twice more.
- Cast off, keeping to the K2, P2 pattern.

MAKING UP
Using mattress stitch, join the back seam of the trousers so that the lowest part of the seam is level with the crotch. Then join the two inside leg seams, again, using mattress stitch.

HAT
The hat is knitted in two main parts – the side band and the tip. The peak is knitted onto the side band once the two main parts have been stitched together.

SIDE BAND
MAKE 1
- Cast on 26 sts in black.
- K 2 rows.
- Break yarn and join mid-blue yarn.
- Next row: P.
- Next row: K1, [inc1] to last st, K1. (50 sts)
- Work 3 rows in st st, beg with a P row.
- Cast off pwise.

TIP
MAKE 1
- Cast on 10 sts in mid-blue.
- 1st row: K1, inc1, K to last 2 sts, inc1, K1. (12 sts)
- Next row: P.
- Next row: K1, M1, K to last st, M1, K1. (14 sts)
- Next row: P.
- Rep last 2 rows 3 times more. (20 sts)
- Work 4 rows in st st, beg with a K row.
- Next row: K1, k2tog, K to last 3 sts, ssk, K1. (18 sts)
- Next row: P.
- Rep last 2 rows 3 times more. (12 sts)
- Next row: K1, k2tog, K to last 3 sts, ssk, K1. (10 sts)
- Cast off kwise.

Join the short sides of the side band to form a circle and oversew the tip in place from the inside, so that the rows of knitting lie across the width of the hat.

PEAK
MAKE 1
- With the RS of the hat facing, using black yarn, pick up and knit 12 sts across the lower edge of the front of the side band, one side to the other.
- Next row: P.
- Next row: K1, k2tog, K to last 3 sts, ssk, K1. (10 sts)
- Next row: P.
- Rep last 2 rows once more. (8 sts)
- Next row: K1, M1, K6, M1, K1. (10 sts)
- Next row: P.
- Next row: K1, M1, K8, M1, K1. (12 sts)
- Cast off kwise.

MAKING UP
Fold the cast-off edge of the peak under. Oversew the sides of the peak together and the cast-off edge of the peak to the inside of the hat. Sew the metal button in place.

BOOT
MAKE 1
- Cast on 30 sts in black.
- K 2 rows.
- Work 4 rows in st st, beg with a K row.
- Next row: K8, cast off 14 sts, K to end. (16 sts)
- Work 7 rows in st st, beg with a P row.
- Next row: P.
- Cast off pwise.

MAKING UP
Fold the piece widthways with the right sides together. Oversew the back, lower and upper seams then turn the boot right side out.

BONE TRUNCHEON
MAKE 1
- Cast on 10 sts in cream.
- Work 2 rows in st st, beg with a K row.
- Next row: K1, k2tog, K4, ssk, K1. (8 sts)
- Work 15 rows in st st, beg with a P row.
- Next row: K1, M1, K6, M1, K1. (10 sts)
- Next row: P.
- Cast off.

MAKING UP
Fold the piece in half lengthways, with the right sides on the inside, and oversew both ends. Turn the bone right side out, insert the plastic drinking straw and sew the seam, using mattress stitch. Make a couple of straight stitches at each short edge to create the bone ends.

Village IdIOT ZOMBIE MASH-UP

Zombie Rock Star head and brain + Zombie Gravedigger head + Frankenstein's Monster upper body + Frankenstein's Monster arms

Frankenstein's Monster jacket

Classic Zombie trousers + Classic Zombie legs =

He may be a couple of cards short of a full deck, but this particular idiot is smart enough to know that two heads are better than one. So he's brought one along with him, clasped securely under his rotten arm. And with his brain (decoratively adorned with chain stitch) sitting loosely in his cranium, he may well need a spare. Every zombie needs one brain to think with and another to eat.

zombie FATaLE

She's pretty well-groomed – for a zombie, that is. Her beehive hairdo is neatly furled and finished with a shiny flower, her crochet dress is set off with a cute pink trim and even if her face is a bit of a battleground, she's still boasting a cheery slash of bright fuchsia lipstick. Under her frock, however, her heart's hanging loose in her chest; the shiny red nails on that single unbandaged hand look a tad like claws – and is that a spider on her ladylike fascinator? Ugh, better not offer to buy this gal a drink.

PEDiGrEE

1897 Bram Stoker's *Dracula* features Lucy Westenra, lovely, intelligent and one of the first female undead, who, after her death, comes back to prey on children. At this date, the label 'undead' still covers a range of options!

1932 The first zombie-themed movie, *White Zombie* (right), is released in the US. It stars Bela Lugosi, and features an alluring femme fatale-style zombie.

2004 *Shaun of the Dead*, an award-winning zombie comedy, offers its audiences an unusually everyday girl zombie in the girl-in-the-garden scene.

SHE WAS NOT ALIVE... NOR DEAD... Just a

WHITE ZOMBIE

Performing his every desire

A VICTOR & EDWARD HALPERIN Production

with BELA Dracula LUGOSI

Released by UNITED ARTISTS

Zombie FaTALE

Although she died a while back, that doesn't mean that she's let herself go. Take a look at her charm-hung belt and you'll get the idea. And with all those boys out in Zombie Land, she could easily lose her heart. No worries: you can pop it right back into her chest.

YOU WILL NEED

70 m/77 yd (28 g/1 oz) pale grey DK yarn

Small amounts of red, pastel pink, white and sparkly black DK yarns

Very small amounts of black, green, cream, dark grey and bright pink DK yarns

Small amounts of yellow and black mohair or mohair/silk yarns

34 m/37 yd (14 g/½ oz) mid-pink DK yarn

9 m/10 yd (4 g/⅛ oz) mauve DK yarn

30 g/1 oz polyester toy filling

Cream sewing thread

Six red bugle beads

A red flower button

A small bronze metal skull charm with jump ring

A small white feather charm with jump ring

A small pale yellow bow

Three 15-mm (⅝-in) brass rings

A piece of black netting measuring 4.5 x 16 cm (1¾ x 6¼ in)

Two 5-mm (¼-in) black beads

A piece of Velcro tape in white, measuring 2.5 x 1 cm (1 x ⅜ in)

A piece of Velcro tape in white, measuring 5 x 2 cm (2 x ¾ in)

Two 13-mm (½-in) snap fasteners

YOU WILL ALSO NEED

A pair of 3 mm (US 2/3) knitting needles

A size 3.25 mm (US D-3) or similar size crochet hook

A yarn needle to sew your items together

An embroidery needle

An ordinary sewing needle

A green crayon

THE DOLL
HEAD
MAKE 2 PIECES
- Cast on 6 sts in pale grey.
- 1st row: Inc1, K to last 2 sts, inc1, K1. (8 sts)
- Next row: P.
- Rep last 2 rows once more. (10 sts)
- Next row: K2, M1, K to last 2 sts, M1, K2. (12 sts)
- Next row: P.
- Rep last 2 rows twice more. (16 sts)
- Work 10 rows in st st, beg with a K row.
- Next row: K2, k2tog, K8, ssk, K2. (14 sts)
- Next row: P2tog, P10, p2tog. (12 sts)
- Cast off.

UPPER BODY
The upper body is knitted from the top to the bottom.

FRONT
MAKE 1
- Cast on 14 sts in pale grey.
- Work 6 rows in st st, beg with a K row.
- Next row: Cast on 4 sts, K to end. (18 sts)
- Next row: Cast on 4 sts, P to end. (22 sts)
- Work 2 rows in st st, beg with a K row.
- Next row: K11, turn and work on these 11 sts only, leaving rem 11 sts on needle.
- Next row: K1, P10.
- Next row: K.
- Next row: K1, P10.
- Rep last 2 rows once more.
- Next row: K4, k2tog, K5. (10 sts)
- Break yarn and rejoin it to rem 11 sts on RS of work.
- Next row: K.
- Next row: P10, K1.

- Rep last 2 rows twice more.
- Next row: K5, ssk, K4. (10 sts)
- Now work across all 20 sts.
- Next row: P2tog, P16, p2tog. (18 sts)
- Work 4 rows in st st, beg with a K row.
- Next row: K4, M1, K to last 4 sts, M1, K2. (20 sts)
- Next row: P.
- Rep last 2 rows once more. (22 sts)
- Work 3 rows in st st, beg with a K row.
- Next row: P4, K14, P4.
- Next row: Cast off 4 sts, K to last 4 sts, cast off 4 sts. (14 sts)
- Break yarn and rejoin it to WS of work.
- Work 5 rows in st st, beg with a P row.
- Cast off.

BACK
MAKE 1
- Cast on 14 sts in pale grey.
- Work 8 rows in st st, beg with a K row.
- Next row: K2, k2tog, K6, ssk, K2. (12 sts)
- Next row: P2tog, P8, p2tog. (10 sts)
- Work 4 rows in st st, beg with a K row.
- Next row: K2, M1, K to last 2 sts, M1, K2. (12 sts)
- Next row: P.
- Rep last 2 rows once more. (14 sts)
- Work 4 rows in st st, beg with a K row.
- Cast off.

LOWER BODY
FRONT
MAKE 1
- Cast on 14 sts in pale grey.

- Work 6 rows in st st, beg with a K row.
- Next row: Cast on 4 sts, K to end. (18 sts)
- Next row: Cast on 4 sts, P to end. (22 sts)
- Work 7 rows in st st, beg with a K row.
- Next row: P4, K14, P4.
- Next row: Cast off 4 sts, K to last 4 sts, cast off 4 sts. (14 sts)
- Break yarn and rejoin it to WS of work.
- Work 5 rows in st st, beg with a P row.
- Cast off.

BACK
MAKE 1
- Cast on 14 sts in pale grey.
- Work 8 rows in st st, beg with a K row.
- Cast off.

CHEST POCKET FOR HEART
MAKE 1
- Cast on 6 sts in pale grey.
- Work 4 rows in st st, beg with a K row.
- Next row: K1, M1, K to last st, M1, K1. (8 sts)
- Work 7 rows in st st, beg with a P row.

- Next row: K1, k2tog, K to last 3 sts, ssk, K1. (6 sts)
- Work 3 rows in st st, beg with a P row.
- Cast off.

HEART
MAKE 1
- Cast on 8 sts in red.
- 1st row: Inc1, K to last 2 sts, inc1, K1. (10 sts)
- Next row: P.
- Rep last 2 rows once more. (12 sts)
- Work 2 rows in st st, beg with a K row.
- Next row: K1, k2tog, K2, k2tog, K2, ssk, K1. (9 sts)
- Next row: P2tog, P5, p2tog. (7 sts)
- Next row: K1, k2tog, K1, ssk, K1. (5 sts)
- Next row: P2tog, P1, p2tog. (3 sts)
- Break yarn and thread it through rem sts.

BLOOD VESSELS
MAKE 2
- Using the crochet hook, work a 2.5-cm (1-in) chain in red for each blood vessel.

LEGS
MAKE 2
- Cast on 26 sts in pale grey.
- Work 5 rows in st st, beg with a K row.
- Next row: P5, cast off 16 sts, P to end. (10 sts)
- Work 20 rows in st st, beg with a K row.
- Cast off.

ARMS
MAKE 2
- Cast on 4 sts in pale grey.
- Work 4 rows in st st, beg with a K row.
- Next row: Cast on 3 sts, K to end. (7 sts)
- Next row: Cast on 3 sts, P to end. (10 sts)

- Work 26 rows in st st, beg with a K row.
- Next row: K1, k2tog, K4, ssk, K1. (8 sts)
- Next row: P2tog, P4, p2tog. (6 sts)
- Break yarn, thread it through rem sts and secure.

MAKING UP & DECORATING
Sew the head, body, arms and legs together, as outlined in the instructions on page 17.

Fold the chest pocket in half widthways, with right sides facing inwards, and oversew the sides together. Oversew the top edges of the pocket to the outer sides of the gap on the upper body, so that the seams of the pocket are at the top and bottom of the gap and the right side of the knitting is on the inside of the pocket.

Fold the heart lengthways so that the right side is facing outwards. Pull the yarn tail from the last row fairly tightly and oversew the side and top seams, stuffing the heart lightly as you go. Thread the tail at one end of the two blood vessels up the chain and pull slightly so that the chain curves. Use the tail ends to sew the blood vessels to the top of the heart.

Using a separated strand of black yarn, work a length of chain stitch for the scar on the leg and work a few straight stitches over the scar. Using a separated strand of bright red yarn, work a length of chain stitch for the scar on the arm and work a few straight stitches over the scar, using a separated strand of black yarn.

Sew three red bugle beads to one arm and one foot to represent nails.

Using black yarn, embroider two French knots for the eyes. Using green yarn, work an oval around one eye and using cream yarn, work an oval around the other eye. Using pale grey yarn, embroider the nose in chain stitch. Using a separated strand of black yarn, work the eyebrows in chain stitch. Using a separated strand of dark grey yarn, work the eyeliner in chain stitch. Using a separated strand of bright pink yarn, work two V-shaped stitches, one over the top of the other, for the mouth. Using a separated strand of red yarn, work the blood trickling from the eye and the scar coming up from the mouth in chain stitch. Work a few straight stitches over the scar, using a separated strand of black yarn. Shade under one eye and on one foot end, using the green crayon.

Cut the yellow mohair yarn for the hair into twenty 70-cm (28-in) lengths and gather together in a bunch. Secure the centre of the lengths to the top of the head and at each side of the face. Take the yarn bunches at the sides back to the top of the head and secure again. Take the hair down the back of the head, spread slightly and back stitch across the head from one side to the other, in line with the stitches that have secured the hair to the sides. Take the hair back up to the top of the head. Wind into an untidy bun and secure. Stitch the red flower button in place. Put the brass ring 'bracelets' on the arms.

DRESS
BACK
MAKE 1
- Cast on 24 sts in pastel pink.
- Break yarn and join mid-pink yarn.

- Next row: P.
- Next row: K2, [yf, k2tog] to last 2 sts, K2.
- Next row: P.
- Next row: K3, [yf, k2tog] to last st, K1.
- Rep last 4 rows 3 times more.
- Next row: P.
- Next row: K2, [yf, k2tog] to last 2 sts, K2.
- Next row: P2tog, P to last 2 sts, p2tog. (22 sts)

the top of each seam to form the armholes. When the dress has been soaked, reshaped and dried (see page 16), put it on the doll. Thread the skull and feather charms onto the belt, wind the belt twice around the doll's waist and secure in a knot.

- Rep last 2 rows 3 times more. (16 sts)
- The lower part of the dress will probably look a little uneven at this stage because of the nature of the stitch pattern. But don't worry – this will be sorted once the dress has been stitched together, soaked and dried (see page 16).
- Next row: K2, [yf, k2tog] to last 2 sts, K2.
- Next row: P.
- Next row: K3, [yf, k2tog] to last st, K1.
- Next row: P. *
- Rep last 4 rows 3 times more.
- K 2 rows.
- Cast off.

FRONT
MAKE 1
- Work as for back until *.
- Rep last 4 rows once more.
- Next row: K2, [yf, k2tog] twice, K2, turn and work on 8 sts just worked only, leaving rem 8 sts on needle.

- Next row: K2, P6.
- Next row: K3, [yf, k2tog] twice, K1.
- Next row: K2, P6.
- Rep last 4 rows once more.
- Next row: K6, ssk. (7 sts)
- Next row: K2tog, K5. (6 sts)
- Cast off.
- Rejoin yarn to rem sts on RS of work.
- Next row: K2, [yf, k2tog] twice, K2. (8 sts)
- Next row: P6, K2.
- Next row: K3, [yf, k2tog] twice, K1.
- Next row: P6, K2.
- Rep last 4 rows once more.
- Next row: K2tog, K6. (7 sts)
- Next row: K5, ssk. (6 sts)
- Cast off.

BELT
MAKE 1
- Using the crochet hook, work a 40-cm (16-in) crochet chain in sparkly black.

MAKING UP
With the right sides of your pieces facing outwards, join the front to the back of the dress at the shoulders. Sew the side seams, using mattress stitch, leaving a gap of 2 cm (¾ in) at

BANDAGE
MAKE 1
- Cast on 11 sts in white.
- Work 14 rows in st st, beg with a K row.
- Next row: K1, k2tog, K5, ssk, K1. (9 sts)
- Next row: P2tog, P5, p2tog. (7 sts)
- Break yarn and thread it through rem sts.

MAKING UP
Pull thread fairly tightly and with the right sides facing outwards sew the side seam, using mattress stitch. Using white yarn, embroider the bandage markings in chain stitch.

SHOE
MAKE 1
- Cast on 10 sts in sparkly black.
- 1st row: Inc1, K to last 2 sts, inc1, K1. (12 sts)
- Next row: P.
- Rep last 2 rows twice more. (16 sts)
- Next row: Inc1, K to last 2 sts, inc1, K1. (18 sts)
- Next row: P7, cast off 4 sts pwise, P to end.
- Work on 7 sts just knitted only, leaving rem sts on needle.
- Work 8 rows in st st, beg with a K row.
- Cast off.

- Break yarn and rejoin it to rem sts on RS of work.
- Work 8 rows in st st, beg with a K row.
- Cast off.

MAKING UP

Fold the shoe piece in half lengthways, with the right sides together, and oversew the back and lower seams. Turn the shoe right side out and then sew on the bow.

HAT

MAKE 1

- Cast on 24 sts in mauve.
- Work 6 rows in st st, beg with a K row.
- Next row: Cast off 10 sts, K4, cast off 10 sts. (4 sts)
- Break yarn and rejoin it to rem sts on WS of work.
- Next row: Inc1 pwise, P1, inc1 pwise, K1. (6 sts)
- Next row: Inc1, K3, inc1, K1. (8 sts)
- Work 3 rows in st st, beg with a P row.
- Next row: K1, k2tog, K2, ssk, K1. (6 sts)
- Next row: P2tog, K2, p2tog. (4 sts)
- Next row: K2tog, ssk. (2 sts)
- Next row: P2tog. (1 st)
- Break yarn and pull it through rem st.
- With RS facing, pick up and K 24 sts along cast-on edge.
- Next row: P.
- Next row: [Inc1] 23 times, K1. (47 sts)
- Work 4 rows in st st, beg with a P row.
- Cast off kwise.

MAKING UP

Join the back seam of the hat, using mattress stitch. Oversew the top part of the hat to the sides from the inside. Using a separated strand of mauve yarn, work a row of running stitch along one long edge of the black netting. Gather it and sew the veil in place just under the brim of the hat, using the same piece of yarn. Round the lower corners of the veil with scissors.

For each of the two spiders, cut four 4-cm (1½-in) lengths of black mohair yarn. Tie the pieces together at the centre with a longer piece of yarn and thread both ends of the longer yarn through the bead. Secure one spider to the brim of the hat so that it hangs down. For the second spider, knot the yarn at the top and take the yarn down through the bead again and use these to secure the spider to the hat. Trim the spiders' legs.

Dracula

Is he a zombie? Hmm. He's undead, that's for sure. But his soigné appearance makes a pleasant change in the motley zombie line-up. Nicely smoothed hair, slick with pomade, a well-cut cape with deep yellow accents, and a neatly fitted waistcoat and trousers all make him stand out in this crowd. Don't be deceived: a great line in sophisticated banter and exceptionally white teeth don't mean that this is company that you should be keeping.

PEDIGREE

1845–7 *Varney the Vampire; or, the Feast of Blood* (right) appears as one of the 'penny dreadful' serials so popular in the nineteenth century.

1897 Bram Stoker's classic *Dracula* is published, introducing the languid sophisticate so familiar to today's vampire enthusiasts.

1931 Bela Lugosi immortalizes Stoker's anti-hero on celluloid, setting the standard for vampires ever since.

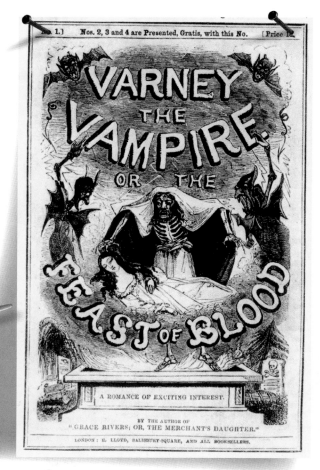

Dracula

With his pointed ears and a cool pet bat, this visitor to Zombie Land survives on the blood of others – and you can see it trickling out of his mouth. Smartly dressed and sporting an elegant skull-topped cane, he may be a cut above your average zombie – though those trousers are looking a mite tattered. In short, he is a great addition to the zombie horde.

YOU WILL NEED

70 m/77 yd (28 g/1 oz) pale green DK yarn

74 m/81 yd (30 g/1 oz) black DK yarn

Very small amounts of white, red and purple DK yarns

23 m/25 yd (9.5 g/⅜ oz) teal DK yarn

19 m/21 yd (8 g/¼ oz) pale grey DK yarn

Small amounts of deep yellow and pale brown DK yarns

Cream sewing thread

30 g/1 oz polyester toy filling

Two small cylindrical white glass beads

Three small grey buttons

A 13.5-cm (5¼-in) length of plastic drinking straw

A skull-shaped plastic button

A piece of Velcro tape in beige, measuring 2.5 x 1 cm (1 x ⅜ in)

A piece of Velcro tape in beige, measuring 5 x 2 cm (2 x ¾ in)

Two 13-mm (½-in) snap fasteners

YOU WILL ALSO NEED

A pair of 3 mm (US 2/3) knitting needles

A size 3.25 mm (US D-3) or similar size crochet hook

A yarn needle to sew your items together

An embroidery needle

An ordinary sewing needle

A grey crayon

THE DOLL

HEAD
FRONT
MAKE 1

- Cast on 4 sts in pale green.
- 1st row: Inc1, K1, inc1, K1. (6 sts)
- Next row: P.
- Next row: K2, M1, K to last 2 sts, M1, K2. (8 sts)
- Next row: P.
- Rep last 2 rows 4 times more. (16 sts) *
- Work 12 rows in st st, beg with a K row.
- Next row: K2, k2tog, K8, ssk, K2. (14 sts)
- Next row: P2tog, P10, p2tog. (12 sts)
- Cast off.

BACK
MAKE 1

- Work as for front until *.
- Work 4 rows in st st, beg with a K row.
- Break yarn and join black yarn.
- Work 8 rows in st st, beg with a K row.
- Next row: K2, k2tog, K8, ssk, K2. (14 sts)
- Next row: P2tog, P10, p2tog. (12 sts)
- Cast off.

FIRST EAR
MAKE 1

- Cast on 4 sts in pale green.
- 1st row: Inc1, K3. (5 sts)
- Next row: P.
- Cast off.

SECOND EAR
MAKE 1

- Cast on 4 sts in pale green.
- 1st row: K3, inc1. (5 sts)
- Next row: P.
- Cast off.

UPPER BODY
The upper body is knitted from the top to the bottom.

FRONT
MAKE 1

- Cast on 14 sts in pale green.
- Work 6 rows in st st, beg with a K row.
- Next row: Cast on 4 sts, K to end. (18 sts)
- Next row: Cast on 4 sts, P to end. (22 sts)
- Work 23 rows in st st, beg with a K row.
- Next row: P4, K14, P4.
- Next row: Cast off 4 sts, K to last 4 sts, cast off 4 sts. (14 sts)
- Break yarn and rejoin it to WS of work.
- Work 5 rows in st st, beg with a P row.
- Cast off.

BACK
MAKE 1

- Cast on 14 sts in pale green.
- Work 24 rows in st st, beg with a K row.
- Cast off.

LOWER BODY
FRONT
MAKE 1

- Cast on 14 sts in pale green.
- Work 6 rows in st st, beg with a K row.
- Next row: Cast on 4 sts, K to end. (18 sts)
- Next row: Cast on 4 sts, P to end. (22 sts)
- Work 7 rows in st st, beg with a K row.
- Next row: P4, K14, P4.
- Next row: Cast off 4 sts, K to last 4 sts, cast off 4 sts. (14 sts)
- Break yarn and rejoin it to RS of work.

- Work 5 rows in st st, beg with a P row.
- Cast off.

BACK
MAKE 1

- Cast on 14 sts in pale green.
- Work 8 rows in st st, beg with a K row.
- Cast off.

LEGS
MAKE 2

- Cast on 28 sts in pale green.
- Work 6 rows in st st, beg with a K row.
- Next row: K6, cast off 16 sts, K to end. (12 sts)
- Work 23 rows in st st, beg with a P row.
- Cast off.

ARMS
MAKE 2

- Cast on 4 sts in pale green.
- Work 4 rows in st st, beg with a K row.
- Next row: Cast on 3 sts, K to end. (7 sts)
- Next row: Cast on 3 sts, P to end. (10 sts)
- Work 28 rows in st st, beg with a K row.
- Next row: K1, k2tog, K4, ssk, K1. (8 sts)
- Next row: P2tog, P4, p2tog. (6 sts)
- Break yarn, thread it through rem sts and secure.

MAKING UP & DECORATING

Sew the head, body, arms and legs together as outlined in the instructions on page 17.

Oversew the ears in place at the sides of the head. Embroider two French knots for the eyes, using black yarn. Using white yarn, work a ring of chain stitch around each French knot. Using a single separated strand of red yarn, work three straight stitches from the centre to the outside of one eye. Using a separated strand of black yarn, work the eyebrows in chain stitch. Embroider the nose in chain stitch, using pale green yarn. Embroider the mouth in chain stitch, using a separated strand of purple yarn. Use a separated strand of red yarn to work the trickles of blood in chain stitch. Sew on the two white glass beads for the teeth.

Shade one of the eye sockets, using the grey crayon.

Using black yarn, work a few rows in chain stitch to form the front part of the hair and sideburns, using the photograph as a guide.

TROUSERS
MAKE 1

- Cast on 19 sts in teal for the first leg.
- 1st row: K2, [yf, s1, k2tog, psso, yf, K1] 4 times, K1.
- Next row: P.
- Next row: K1, k2tog, yf, K1, [yf, s1, k2tog, psso, yf, K1] 3 times, yf, s1, K1, psso, K1.

- Next row: P.
- Rep last 4 rows once more.
- Work 4 rows in st st, beg with a K row.
- Break yarn and leave sts on needle.
- Cast on 19 sts for second leg.
- Work 18 rows in st st, beg with a K row.
- Next row: K 19 sts from second leg, then 19 sts from first leg. (38 sts)
- Work 15 rows in st st, beg with a P row.
- Next row: [K2, P2] 9 times.
- Next row: [P2, K2] 9 times.
- Next row: [K2, P2] 9 times.
- Cast off, keeping to the K2, P2 pattern.

MAKING UP

Using mattress stitch, join the back seam of the trousers so that the lowest part of the seam is level with the crotch. Then join the two inside leg seams, again using mattress stitch.

WAISTCOAT
MAKE 1

- Cast on 42 sts in pale grey.
- 1st row: K2, P to last 2 sts, K2.
- Next row: K.
- Rep last 2 rows 5 times more.
- Next row: K2, P to last 2 sts, K2.
- Next row: K11, turn and work on these 11 sts only, leaving rem 31 sts on needle.
- Next row: K2, P7, K2. (11 sts)
- Next row: K2, k2tog, K to end. (10 sts)
- Next row: K2, P to last 2 sts, K2.
- Rep last 2 rows 4 times more. (6 sts)
- Next row: K.
- Next row: K2, P2, K2.
- Cast off and break yarn.

- Rejoin yarn to sts rem on needle on RS of work.
- Next row: K20, turn and work on these 20 sts only, leaving rem 11 sts on needle.
- Next row: K2, P16, K2.
- Next row: K.
- Rep last 2 rows 5 times more.
- Next row: K.
- Cast off and break yarn.
- Rejoin yarn to 11 sts rem on needle on RS of work.
- Next row: K. (11 sts)
- Next row: K2, P7, K2.
- Next row: K to last 4 sts, ssk, K2. (10 sts)
- Next row: K2, P to last 2 sts, K2.
- Rep last 2 rows 4 times more. (6 sts)
- Next row: K.
- Next row: K2, P2, K2.
- Cast off.

MAKING UP

With the right sides of the waistcoat together, oversew the shoulder seams. Overlap the left border over the right border of the waistcoat and sew on the small grey buttons.

CLOAK
MAKE 1

- Cast on 28 sts in black.
- K 2 rows.
- Next row: K6, M1, K2, M1, K12, M1, K2, M1, K6. (32 sts)
- Next and every WS row unless stated: P.
- Next RS row: K7, M1, K2, M1, K14, M1, K2, M1, K7. (36 sts)
- Next RS row: K8, M1, K2, M1, K16, M1, K2, M1, K8. (40 sts)
- Next RS row: K9, M1, K2, M1, K18, M1, K2, M1, K9. (44 sts)
- Next RS row: K10, M1, K2, M1, K20, M1, K2, M1, K10. (48 sts)

- Next RS row: K11, M1, K2, M1, K22, M1, K2, M1, K11. (52 sts)
- Next row: P.
- Work 30 rows in st st, beg with a K row.
- K 2 rows.
- Cast off pwise.

- With RS facing, pick up and K 28 sts across top (neck) edge.
- K 14 rows.
- Cast off.

TIES
MAKE 2
- Using the crochet hook, make a 16-cm (6½-in) chain in deep yellow for each cloak tie.

MAKING UP
Weave the yarn tail at one end of each of the ties back into the chain and trim. Use the other yarn tail to secure the tie to the neck edges of the cloak.

CANE
MAKE 1
- Cast on 38 sts in pale brown.
- Work 3 rows in st st, beg with a K row.
- Cast off pwise.

MAKING UP
Roll the piece around your length of drinking straw so that the reverse of the stocking stitch is on the outside. Oversew down the long seam and the two ends. Sew the skull button in place.

Bat

THE DOLL
BODY
MAKE 1
- Cast on 4 sts in black.
- 1st row: [Inc1, K1] twice. (6 sts)
- Next row: P.
- Next row: K1, M1, K4, M1, K1. (8 sts)
- Work 5 rows in st st, beg with a P row.
- Next row: K1, k2tog, K2, ssk, K1. (6 sts)
- Next row: P.
- Next row: K1, k2tog, ssk, K1. (4 sts)
- Next row: [P2tog] twice. (2 sts)
- Next row: K2tog.
- Break yarn and pull it through rem st.

WINGS
The wings are knitted from the lower edge to the top edge.
MAKE 2
- Cast on 20 sts in black.
- 1st row: P2tog, P16, p2tog. (18 sts)
- Next row: K4, p2tog, K6, p2tog, K4. (16 sts)
- Next row: P4, k2tog, P4, k2tog, P4. (14 sts)
- Next row: K2tog, K2, p2tog, K2, p2tog, K2, k2tog. (10 sts)
- Next row: P2tog, k2tog, P2, k2tog, p2tog. (6 sts)
- Next row: K2tog, K2, k2tog. (4 sts)
- Next row: [P2tog] twice. (2 sts)
- Next row: S1, K1, psso. (1 st)
- Break yarn and pull it through rem st.

EARS
MAKE 2
- Cast on 3 sts in black.
- Work 2 rows in st st, beg with a K row.
- Next row: S1, k2tog, psso. (1 st)
- Break yarn and pull it through rem st.

MAKING UP
Fold the body piece in half lengthways, with right side facing outwards, and join the body seam, stuffing the body slightly as you go. Stitch the ears in place. Stitch the lower side parts of the wings to the body, using the photograph as a guide.

Mother of the BRiDE

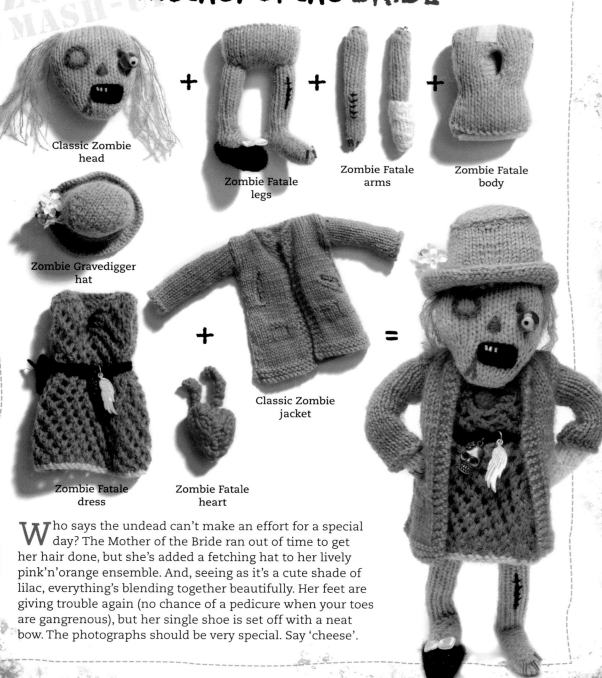

Classic Zombie head

Zombie Fatale legs

Zombie Fatale arms

Zombie Fatale body

Zombie Gravedigger hat

Zombie Fatale dress

Zombie Fatale heart

Classic Zombie jacket

W ho says the undead can't make an effort for a special day? The Mother of the Bride ran out of time to get her hair done, but she's added a fetching hat to her lively pink'n'orange ensemble. And, seeing as it's a cute shade of lilac, everything's blending together beautifully. Her feet are giving trouble again (no chance of a pedicure when your toes are gangrenous), but her single shoe is set off with a neat bow. The photographs should be very special. Say 'cheese'.

zombie CHeF

His razor-sharp batterie de cuisine marks this guy out as a professional, whatever his undead status. And he's got the kit to match – jaunty moustache, chequered trousers and a full set of 'whites'. You have to wonder what it is he's been cooking, though, for them to get in such a state. What a lot of stains – even boiling will never get them out! Could it be that he's transformed himself into a one-zombie conversion unit?

PEDiGrEE

1934 The Zombie first enters the dining sphere – with a cocktail. Invented by Donn Beach, an early celebrity restaurateur, the brandy and rum-based drink (left) doesn't turn drinkers into zombies – they just feel that way.

1986 The clunkingly named *Gore-met* is, perhaps surprisingly, the first movie that starred an out-and-out cannibal zombie chef.

1997 The infamous cafeteria zombie scene is aired during the first season of the satirical cartoon, *South Park*: school lunches will never seem the same again.

Zombie Chef

If you were in any doubt at all that you wouldn't much like this chef preparing your supper, take a look at those horrible black fingernails. Splashed in blood and goodness knows what else, he's always at the ready with his knife and cleaver to do a little emergency surgery should you be unwise enough to get up close and personal.

YOU WILL NEED

70 m/77 yd (28 g/1 oz) light grey DK yarn

Small amounts of red and dark brown DK yarns

52 m/57 yd (21 g/¾ oz) white DK yarn

Very small amounts of black, bright pink, pale green and dark grey DK yarns

Very small amount of black mohair or mohair/silk yarn

15 m/16½ yd (4 g/⅛ oz) navy 4-ply yarn

13 m/14½ yd (3.5 g/⅛ oz) cream 4-ply yarn

Small amount of dark grey metallic crochet yarn

30 g/1 oz polyester toy filling

Cream sewing thread

Six black bugle beads

A small gold bead

Four small black buttons

A small piece of stiff grey or silver card

A piece of Velcro tape in white, measuring 2.5 x 1 cm (1 x ⅜ in)

A piece of Velcro tape in white, measuring 5 x 2 cm (2 x ¾ in)

Two 13-mm (½-in) snap fasteners

YOU WILL ALSO NEED

A pair of 3 mm (US 2/3) knitting needles

A pair of 2.75 mm (US 2) knitting needles

Stitch holder or spare needle

A yarn needle to sew your items together

An embroidery needle

An ordinary sewing needle

A green crayon

THE DOLL
HEAD
MAKE 2 PIECES
- Using 3 mm (US 2/3) needles, cast on 10 sts in light grey.
- 1st row: Inc1, K7, inc1, K1. (12 sts)
- Next row: P.
- Next row: K2, M1, K8, M1, K2. (14 sts)
- Work 17 rows in st st, beg with a P row.
- Next row: K2, k2tog, K6, ssk, K2. (12 sts)
- Next row: P2tog, P8, p2tog. (10 sts)
- Cast off.

INNER FACE
MAKE 1 PIECE
- Using 3 mm (US 2/3) needles, cast on 10 sts in red.
- 1st row: Inc1, K7, inc1, K1. (12 sts)
- Next row: P.
- Next row: K2, M1, K8, M1, K2. (14 sts)
- Work 17 rows in st st, beg with a P row.
- Next row: K2, k2tog, K6, ssk, K2. (12 sts)
- Next row: P2tog, P8, p2tog. (10 sts)
- Cast off.

EARS
MAKE 2
- Using 3 mm (US 2/3) needles, cast on 5 sts in light grey.
- 1st row: K.
- Next row: P2tog, K1, p2tog. (3 sts)
- Next row: S1, k2tog, psso.
- Break yarn and pull it through rem st.

UPPER BODY
The upper body is knitted from the top to the bottom.
FRONT
MAKE 1
- Using 3 mm (US 2/3) needles, cast on 14 sts in light grey.
- Work 6 rows in st st, beg with a K row.
- Next row: Cast on 4 sts, K to end. (18 sts)
- Next row: Cast on 4 sts, P to end. (22 sts)
- Work 23 rows in st st, beg with a K row.
- Next row: P4, K14, P4.
- Next row: Cast off 4 sts, K to last 4 sts, cast off 4 sts. (14 sts)
- Break yarn and rejoin it to WS of work.
- Work 5 rows in st st, beg with a P row.
- Cast off.

BACK
MAKE 1
- Using 3 mm (US 2/3) needles, cast on 14 sts in light grey.
- Work 24 rows in st st, beg with a K row.
- Cast off.

LOWER BODY
FRONT
MAKE 1
- Using 3 mm (US 2/3) needles, cast on 14 sts in light grey.

- Work 6 rows in st st, beg with a K row.
- Next row: Cast on 4 sts, K to end. (18 sts)
- Next row: Cast on 4 sts, P to end. (22 sts)
- Work 7 rows in st st, beg with a K row.
- Next row: P4, K14, P4.
- Next row: Cast off 4 sts, K to last 4 sts, cast off 4 sts. (14 sts)
- Break yarn and rejoin it to WS of work.
- Work 5 rows in st st, beg with a P row.
- Cast off.

BACK
MAKE 1
- Using 3 mm (US 2/3) needles, cast on 14 sts in light grey.
- Work 8 rows in st st, beg with a K row.
- Cast off.

FIRST LEG
MAKE 1
- Using 3 mm (US 2/3) needles, cast on 30 sts in light grey.
- Work 6 rows in st st, beg with a K row.
- Next row: K6, cast off 18 sts, K to end. (12 sts) *
- Work 3 rows in st st, beg with a P row.
- Next row: K4, turn and work on these 4 sts only, leaving rem 8 sts on needle.
- Work 6 rows in st st, beg with a P row.
- Break yarn and rejoin to rem 8 sts on RS of work.
- Work 7 rows in st st, beg with a K row.
- Now work over all 12 sts.
- Work 13 rows in st st, beg with a P row.
- Cast off.

SECOND LEG
MAKE 1
- Work as for first leg until *.
- Work 23 rows in st st, beg with a P row.
- Cast off.

BONE
MAKE 1
- Using size 2.75 mm (US 2) needles, cast on 7 sts in white.
- Work 12 rows in st st, beg with a K row.
- Cast off.

ARMS
MAKE 2
- Using 3 mm (US 2/3) needles, cast on 4 sts in light grey.
- Work 4 rows in st st, beg with a K row.
- Next row: Cast on 3 sts, K to end. (7 sts)
- Next row: Cast on 3 sts, P to end. (10 sts)
- Work 28 rows in st st, beg with a K row.
- Next row: K1, k2tog, K4, ssk, K1. (8 sts)
- Next row: P2tog, P4, p2tog. (6 sts)
- Break yarn, thread it through rem sts and secure.

MAKING UP & DECORATING
Sew the body, arms and legs together as outlined in the instructions on page 17.

Fold the bone in half lengthways, so that the right side is on the outside. Oversew one of the short seams and the long seam. Stuff lightly and oversew the second short seam. Work a couple of stitches in the centre of the short seam to make the bone end. Insert the bone into the gap in the leg. Overstitch it in light grey and work a few straight stitches across the bone where it meets the knitted flesh. Using a separated strand of red yarn, work a row of chain stitch down the side and underneath the protruding bone for the wound. Using a separated strand of black yarn, work a few straight stitches over the wound. Sew the black bugle beads in place on the arms for the fingernails.

For the head, place the two main head pieces right sides together. Place the red inner head piece face down on top of the two head pieces. Oversew around the edges of the head, using grey yarn and leaving a gap at one side of the head for turning and stuffing. Turn the head right side out. Because the head is made from three layers rather than two, you will have two 'pockets'. Make sure you stuff the section made up of the back of the head and the red inner part, so that the right side of the red inner part is facing towards the outside. Using red yarn, oversew the gap closed, so that the stuffing is held in but the side section of the front of the face is free to curl back. Using a separated strand of black yarn, work three straight stitches over the curled back edge of the face. Complete the head as outlined in the main instructions.

Oversew the ears in place.

Using black yarn, work two French knots for the eyes. Work an oval of chain stitches around

the French knots, using white yarn. Work a few straight stitches in black mohair yarn for the eyebrows. Work the nose in chain stitch, using light grey yarn. Work a few French knots in light grey yarn on one of the cheeks. Work the outline of the mouth in chain stitch, using a separated strand of bright pink yarn. Work the centre of the mouth in satin stitch, using black yarn and keeping your stitches vertical. Work a couple of straight stitches for the teeth, using pale green yarn. Work the moustache in chain stitch, using a separated strand of dark grey yarn. Sew the gold bead in place for the earring.

Shade under the eyes, using the green crayon.

JACKET

MAKE 1

- Using 3 mm (US 2/3) needles, cast on 42 sts in white.
- K 2 rows.
- Next row: K2, P38, K2.
- Next row: K.
- Rep last 2 rows 9 times more.
- Next row: K2, P38, K2.
- Next row: K13, turn and work on these sts only, leaving rem sts on needle.
- Next row: P11, K2.
- Next row: K.
- Rep last 2 rows twice more.
- Break yarn and leave sts on needle.
- Rejoin yarn to rem sts on RS of work.
- Next row: K16, turn and work on these 16 sts only.
- Work 6 rows in st st, beg with a P row.
- Break yarn and leave sts on needle.
- Rejoin yarn to rem 13 sts on RS of work.
- Next row: K.
- Next row: K2, P11.
- Next row: K.

- Rep last 2 rows twice more.
- Now work across all 42 sts on needle.
- Next row: Cast off 7 sts pwise, K5 (6 sts on needle incl st rem from casting off), [k2tog] 3 times, K4, [ssk] 3 times, K13. (29 sts)
- Next row: Cast off 7 sts, K to end. (22 sts)
- Next row: K.
- Next row: K2tog, K18, ssk. (20 sts)
- Cast off.

SLEEVES

MAKE 2

- Using 3 mm (US 2/3) needles, cast on 14 sts in white.
- 1st row: K.
- Work 24 rows in st st, beg with a K row.
- Cast off.

MAKING UP

With the right sides of the jacket together, oversew the shoulder seams. Join the sleeve seams, using mattress stitch. Insert the sleeves into the armholes of the main piece and oversew them from the inside. Then overlap the right side of the jacket with the left. Sew on three of the buttons and sew the fourth button leaving a longer stem of thread so that it looks as if the button is falling off. Using red yarn, work a combination of French knots, some with straight stitches coming out in a star pattern, to represent splattered blood.

TOQUE

MAKE 1

- Using 3 mm (US 2/3) needles, cast on 30 sts in white.
- K 5 rows.
- Next row: K1, [inc1, K1] to last st, K1. (44 sts)
- Work 13 rows in st st, beg with a P row.
- Next row: [P2tog] 22 times. (22 sts)
- Next row: [K2tog] 11 times. (11 sts)
- Break yarn and thread through rem sts.

MAKING UP

Pull the yarn up fairly firmly and join the seam, using mattress stitch. Distress both the toque and the jacket, using a solution of black tea as described on page 78.

TROUSERS

The trousers are knitted using two colours of yarn – navy and cream 4-ply.

MAKE 1

• Using 3 mm (US 2/3) needles, cast on 22 sts in navy 4-ply for first leg.
• 1st row: [K1 navy, K1 cream] 11 times.
• Next row: [P1 cream, P1 navy] 11 times.
• Rep last 2 rows 9 times more and leave sts on stitch holder or spare needle.
• Cast on 22 sts in navy 4-ply for second leg.
• 1st row: [K1 navy, K1 cream] 11 times.
• Next row: [P1 cream, P1 navy] 11 times.
• Rep last 2 rows 4 times more.
• Now work across all 40 sts.
• Work 14 rows in st st, beg with a K row, keeping to the navy/cream pattern.
• Break cream and cont in navy only.
• K 4 rows.
• Cast off.

MAKING UP

Using mattress stitch, join the back seam of the trousers so that the lowest part of the seam is level with the crotch. Then join the two inside leg seams, again using mattress stitch.

CLEAVER

MAKE 1

• Using 2.75 mm (US 2) needles, cast on 14 sts in dark grey metallic crochet yarn.
• Work 11 rows in st st, beg with a K row.
• Next row: Cast off 4 sts, K5 (6 sts on needles incl st rem from casting off), cast off 4 sts. (6 sts)
• Break yarn and join dark brown yarn to RS of work.
• K 2 rows.
• Work 9 rows in st st, beg with a K row.
• Next row: K.
• Cast off.

MAKING UP

Cut a piece of card, using the template shown above on the left. Fold the cleaver piece in half lengthways, with the right side facing outwards, and oversew it around the card template.

KNIFE

MAKE 1

• Using 2.75 mm (US 2) needles, cast on 6 sts in dark brown.
• 1st row: K.
• Work 11 rows in st st, beg with a K row.
• Next row: K.
• Break yarn and join dark grey metallic crochet yarn to RS of work.
• Work 12 rows in st st, beg with a K row.
• Next row: K2 tog, K2, ssk. (4 sts)
• Next row: [P2tog] twice. (2 sts)
• Break yarn and thread it through rem sts.

MAKING UP

Cut a piece of card, using the template shown above on the right. Fold the knife piece in half lengthways, with the right side facing outwards, and oversew it around the card template.

Biker Chick ZOMBIE

ZOMBIE MASH-UP

Zombie Fatale
head

+

Zombie Fatale
legs

+

Zombie Rock Star
body

+

Zombie Rock Star
arms

Zombie Rock Star
jacket

Zombie Cop
cap

+

Zombie Rock Star
jeans

=

If you're a devotee of the early road movie, Biker Chick Zombie will roll your wheels. She's got all the glamour and quite a bit of the grease of her biker brothers – and with her cap tipped well forward, Brando-style, you could easily mistake her for Marlon's deader sister. Cooler. In every sense.

zombie GRaVEDIGGER

Being a zombie is an equal-opportunities business – there's no reason why gravedigging should be left to the guys. Although this lady is in a very advanced state of putrefaction, she's hanging onto her flowerpot hat. And she's in a growing business; you know that part in the horror movie when the graves all start heaving with their freshly dead occupants? It's a job to free them up to do their gruesome work – and that's why she needs the shovel.

PEDIGREE

1786 Ghouls – creatures found in Eastern myth, who live on newly dead human flesh and frequent graveyards – get their first mention in the novel *Vathek*, by author Samuel Beckford.

C.1900 The *calavera* (skull) prints (right) of the Mexican artist José Posada show skeletons engaged in everyday activities – and gain international popularity.

2011 Fantasy fiction moves right up to date with the publication of the fantasy/crime series, *iZombie*, featuring a detective who is also a (female) gravedigging zombie.

Zombie GraVEDigGER

With a rope and spade, the zombie gravedigger is a specialist at freeing up the undead. Well someone's got to do the job! The monochrome colours and green, maggoty eye may not be immediately enchanting, but she still enjoys her accessories – her hat is decorated with the once-beautiful flowers from some poor soul's grave.

YOU WiLL NEED

70 m/77 yd (28 g/1 oz) dark grey DK yarn

Very small amount of pale green DK yarn

8 m/9 yd (3.5 g/⅛ oz) cream DK yarn

18 m/20 yd (7.5 g/¼ oz) lilac DK yarn

Small amounts of mid-pink, flecked light brown and teal DK yarns

Small amount of dark metallic silver crochet yarn

30 g/1 oz polyester toy filling

Cream sewing thread

One glass bead for the eye

Three 3-mm (⅛-in) white glass teardrop beads

A flower spray with wired stem

A small piece of stiff grey or silver card

A plastic drinking straw

Some sticky tape

A piece of Velcro tape in black measuring 2.5 x 1 cm (1 x ⅜ in)

A piece of Velcro tape in black measuring 5 x 2 cm (2 x ¾ in)

Two 13-mm (½-in) snap fasteners

YOU WILL ALSO NEED

A pair of 3 mm (US 2/3) knitting needles

A pair of 2.75 mm (US 2) knitting needles

A size 3.25 mm (US D-3) or similar size crochet hook

A yarn needle to sew your items together

An embroidery needle

An ordinary sewing needle

THE DOLL
HEAD
MAKE 2 PIECES
- Using 3 mm (US 2/3) needles, cast on 10 sts in dark grey.
- Work 8 rows in st st, beg with a K row.
- Next row: K2, M1, K to last 2 sts, M1, K2. (12 sts)
- Next row: P.
- Rep last 2 rows twice more. (16 sts)
- Work 10 rows in st st, beg with a K row.
- Next row: K2, k2tog, K8, ssk, K2. (14 sts)
- Next row: P2tog, P10, p2tog. (12 sts)
- Cast off.

UPPER BODY
The upper body is knitted from the top to the bottom.
FRONT
MAKE 1
- Using 3 mm (US 2/3) needles, cast on 14 sts in dark grey.
- Work 6 rows in st st, beg with a K row.
- Next row: Cast on 4 sts, K to end. (18 sts)
- Next row: Cast on 4 sts, P to end. (22 sts)
- Work 23 rows in st st, beg with a K row.
- Next row: P4, K14, P4.
- Next row: Cast off 4 sts, K to last 4 sts, cast off 4 sts. (14 sts)
- Break yarn and rejoin it to WS of work.
- Work 5 rows in st st, beg with a P row.
- Cast off.

BACK
MAKE 1
- Using 3 mm (US 2/3) needles, cast on 14 sts in dark grey.

- Work 24 rows in st st, beg with a K row.
- Cast off.

LOWER BODY
FRONT
MAKE 1
- Using 3 mm (US 2/3) needles, cast on 14 sts in dark grey.
- Work 6 rows in st st, beg with a K row.
- Next row: Cast on 4 sts, K to end. (18 sts)
- Next row: Cast on 4 sts, P to end. (22 sts)
- Work 7 rows in st st, beg with a K row.
- Next row: P4, K14, P4.
- Next row: Cast off 4 sts, K to last 4 sts, cast off 4 sts. (14 sts)
- Break yarn and rejoin it to WS of work.
- Work 5 rows in st st, beg with a P row.
- Cast off.

BACK
MAKE 1
- Using 3 mm (US 2/3) needles, cast on 14 sts in dark grey.
- Work 8 rows in st st, beg with a K row.
- Cast off.

LEGS
MAKE 2
- Using 3 mm (US 2/3) needles, cast on 30 sts in dark grey.
- Work 6 rows in st st, beg with a K row.
- Next row: K6, cast off 18 sts, K to end. (12 sts)
- Work 23 rows in st st, beg with a P row.
- Cast off.

ARMS
MAKE 2
- Using 3 mm (US 2/3) needles, cast on 4 sts in dark grey.
- Work 4 rows in st st, beg with a K row.
- Next row: Cast on 3 sts, K to end. (7 sts)
- Next row: Cast on 3 sts, P to end. (10 sts)
- Work 28 rows in st st, beg with a K row.
- Next row: K1, k2tog, K4, ssk, K1. (8 sts)
- Next row: P2tog, P4, p2tog. (6 sts)
- Break yarn, thread it through rem sts and secure.

MAGGOTS
MAKE 3
Using the crochet hook, work a 1-cm (³⁄₈-in) crochet chain for each maggot, using pale green yarn.

MAKING UP & DECORATING
Sew the head, body arms and legs together as outlined in the instructions on page 17.

Using cream yarn, embroider the bones, ribs and skull in chain stitch, using both the main photo and the body parts close-ups (above) to guide you. The knee caps are formed from a small circle of chain stitches. Add straight stitches to the spine to represent the vertebrae and across the beginning of the foot.

Work one eye socket in chain stitch, using cream yarn. Thread the yarn tail at one end of each maggot up through the crochet chain and pull slightly to make the maggot curl. Use the yarn tails to secure the maggots to the eye socket. Attach the glass bead for the second eye and work a few rows of chain stitch around the eye, using cream yarn. Work three straight stitches in cream yarn to form a triangle for the nose. Work a straight stitch in cream yarn for the mouth and attach the three white teardrop beads for the teeth.

HAT
SIDE & RIM
MAKE 1
- Using 3 mm (US 2/3) needles, cast on 35 sts in lilac.
- Work 14 rows in st st, beg with a K row.
- Cast off.
- With RS facing, pick up and knit 35 sts along cast-on edge.
- Next row: P.
- Next row: K1, [inc1] 33 times, K1. (68 sts)
- Work 2 rows in st st, beg with a P row.
- Cast off kwise.

TIP
MAKE 1
- Using 3 mm (US 2/3) needles, cast on 7 sts in lilac.
- 1st row: Inc1, K4, inc1, K1. (9 sts)
- Next row: P.
- Next row: K1, M1, K to last st, M1, K1. (11 sts)
- Next row: P.

- Rep last 2 rows twice more. (15 sts)
- Next row: K1, k2tog, K to last 3 sts, ssk, K1. (13 sts)
- Next row: P.
- Rep last 2 rows twice more. (9 sts)
- Next row: K1, k2tog, K3, ssk, K1. (7 sts)
- Cast off pwise.

MAKING UP
Join the back seam of the side and rim of the hat, using mattress stitch. Oversew the tip of the hat to the sides, working from the inside. Wrap the mid-pink yarn around the hat to represent the hatband and secure. Wrap the wired stem of the flower around the yarn hatband.

ROPE
MAKE 1
- Using the crochet hook, work a 60-cm (2-ft) crochet chain, using flecked light brown yarn.

SPADE
BLADE
MAKE 2 PIECES
- Using 2.75 mm (US 2) needles, cast on 14 sts in metallic silver crochet yarn.
- Work 10 rows in st st, beg with a K row.
- Next row: K1, k2tog, K8, ssk, k1. (12 sts)
- Next row: P.
- Next row: K1, k2tog, K6, ssk, K1. (10 sts)
- Next row: P2tog, P6, p2tog. (8 sts)
- Next row: K1, k2tog, K2, ssk, K1. (6 sts)
- Next row: P2tog, K2, p2tog. (4 sts)
- Next row: [K2tog] twice. (2 sts)
- Next row: P2tog.
- Break yarn and pull through rem st.

HANDLE
MAKE 1
- Using 2.75 mm (US 2) needles, cast on 28 sts in teal.
- Work 3 rows in st st, beg with a K row.
- Cast off kwise.

MAKING UP
Place the two blade pieces together, with the right sides facing outwards. Oversew the two sides, leaving the top edge open. Cut a piece of card, using the template shown to the right. Cut the drinking straw into a 10-cm (4-in) length. Trim the last 1 cm (⅜ in) of the end of the drinking straw into a V-shaped point and make two 1-cm (⅜-in) slits from the sides of the point.

Place the card blade between the pointed ends of the straw and secure with sticky tape. Insert the card into the knitted blade and sew the top edges up to the sides of the handle. Wrap the knitted handle around the straw, so that the reverse of the stocking stitch is on the outside, and oversew the long seam, starting from the top end. Secure the handle to the top of the blade with teal yarn and work a long V shape on each side of the blade, using chain stitch. Fill in with a few straight stitches.

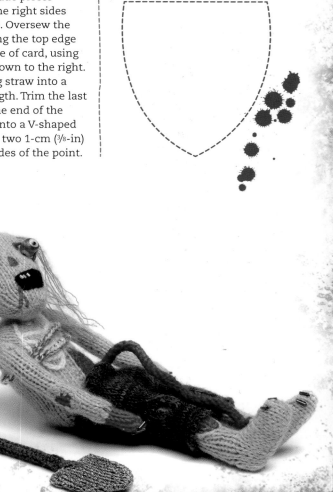

Zombie Rock Star

Flamboyant hair, plenty of chains and a broad, toothy smile: too bad his brains were half fried even before the zombie plague caught him. Still, if they get uncomfortable, they're only loosely attached to the rest of him. Even if he's undead, the star in him is determined to play on – there are still fans to satisfy. And if you don't fancy knitting a rock star, he can easily be converted to the undead leader of a biker gang: just embroider a skull-and-crossbones on the back of his jacket.

PEDIGREE

1985 Inspired by the 1932 movie, the musician and film director Rob Zombie names his heavy metal band White Zombie (right).

2000 *Wild Zero*, surely one of the oddest cult movies ever – a combination of Japanese garage rock, aliens and zombies – wins several awards in the horror/comedy categories on the independent circuit.

2005 Renee Cooper launches her act, Zombie Girl. No reason for all zombie rockers to be male.

zombie RoCK STaR

This stomping zombie has toned down his fast-paced lifestyle just a little since he left the land of the living. The very best thing about him is that you can arrange his hair in a variety of fetching styles – try out a Mohican by taking out his brain and tucking most of the hair, except for the ends, inside the brain pouch. And there are plenty of other possibilities . . .

YOU WiLL NEED

70 m/77 yd (28 g/1 oz) light beige DK yarn

Small amounts of pale pink, red, mid-pink, green, fuzzy light brown and cream DK yarns

Very small amounts of black and white DK yarns

38 m/42 yd (15 g/½ oz) sparkly black DK yarn

25 m/27½ yd (6.5 g/¼ oz) denim blue 4-ply yarn

13 m/14½ yd (5.5 g/¼ oz) dark brown DK yarn

Cream sewing thread

30 g/1 oz polyester toy filling

A silver skull charm

A metal snake charm

A 24-cm (9½-in) length of waxed black cord

A small blue button

A 26-cm (10¼-in) length of silver metal chain

A piece of Velcro tape in beige, measuring 2.5 x 1 cm (1 x ⅜ in)

A piece of Velcro tape in beige, measuring 5 x 2 cm (2 x ¾ in)

Two 13-mm (½-in) snap fasteners

YOU WiLL ALSO NEED

A pair of 3 mm (US 2/3) knitting needles

A pair of 2.75 mm (US 2) knitting needles

A yarn needle to sew your items together

An embroidery needle

An ordinary sewing needle

A grey crayon

THE DOLL

HEAD
MAKE 2 PIECES
- Using 3 mm (US 2/3) needles, cast on 18 sts in pale green.
- 1st row: Inc1, K15, inc1, K1. (20 sts)
- Work 3 rows in st st, beg with a P row.
- Next row: K2, k2tog, K to last 4 sts, ssk, K2. (18 sts)
- Work 3 rows in st st, beg with a P row.
- Rep last 4 rows once more. (16 sts)
- Work 10 rows in st st, beg with a K row.
- Next row: K2, k2tog, K8, ssk, K2. (14 sts)
- Next row: P2tog, P10, p2tog. (12 sts)
- Cast off.

BRAIN POCKET
MAKE 1
- Using 3 mm (US 2/3) needles, cast on 12 sts in light beige.
- Work 4 rows in st st, beg with a K row.
- Next row: K2, M1, K8, M1, K2. (14 sts)
- Work 13 rows in st st, beg with a P row.
- Next row: K2, k2tog, K to last 4 sts, ssk, K2. (12 sts)
- Work 3 rows in st st, beg with a P row.
- Cast off.

BRAIN
MAKE 2 PIECES
- Using size 2.75 mm (US 2) needles, cast on 5 sts in pale pink.
- 1st row: Inc1, K to last 2 sts, inc1, K1. (7 sts)
- Next row: P.

- Rep last 2 rows twice more. (11 sts)
- Work 4 rows in st st, beg with a K row.
- Next row: K1, k2tog, K to last 3 sts, ssk, K1. (9 sts)
- Next row: P.
- Rep last 2 rows once more. (7 sts)
- Next row: K1, k2tog, K1, ssk, K1. (5 sts)
- Cast off kwise.

UPPER BODY
The upper body is knitted from the top to the bottom.

FRONT
MAKE 1
- Using 3 mm (US 2/3) needles, cast on 20 sts in light beige.
- Work 6 rows in st st, beg with a K row.
- Next row: Cast on 4 sts, K to end. (24 sts)
- Next row: Cast on 4 sts, P to end. (28 sts)
- Work 6 rows in st st, beg with a K row.
- Next row: K4, k2tog, K to last 6 sts, ssk, K4. (26 sts)
- Work 5 rows in st st, beg with a P row.
- Rep last 6 rows twice more. (22 sts)
- Next row: K.
- Next row: P4, K14, P4.
- Next row: Cast off 4 sts, K to last 4 sts, cast off 4 sts. (14 sts)
- Break yarn and rejoin it to WS of work.
- Work 5 rows in st st, beg with a P row.
- Cast off.

BACK
MAKE 1
- Using 3 mm (US 2/3) needles, cast on 20 sts in light beige.

- Work 4 rows in st st, beg with a K row.
- Next row: K2, k2tog, K to last 4 sts, ssk, K2. (18 sts)
- Work 5 rows in st st, beg with a P row.
- Rep last 6 rows twice more. (14 sts)
- Cast off.

LOWER BODY
FRONT
MAKE 1
- Using 3 mm (US 2/3) needles, cast on 14 sts in light beige.
- Work 6 rows in st st, beg with a K row.
- Next row: Cast on 4 sts, K to end. (18 sts)
- Next row: Cast on 4 sts, P to end. (22 sts)
- Work 7 rows in st st, beg with a K row.
- Next row: P4, K14, P4.

- Break yarn and rejoin it to WS of work.
- Work 5 rows in st st, beg with a P row.
- Cast off.

BACK
MAKE 1
- Using 3 mm (US 2/3) needles, cast on 14 sts in light beige.
- Work 8 rows in st st, beg with a K row.
- Cast off.

LEGS
MAKE 2
- Using 3 mm (US 2/3) needles, cast on 28 sts in light beige.
- Work 6 rows in st st, beg with a K row.
- Next row: K6, cast off 16 sts, K to end. (12 sts)
- Work 21 rows in st st, beg with a P row.
- Cast off.

ARMS
MAKE 2
- Using 3 mm (US 2/3) needles,

cast on 4 sts in light beige.
- Work 4 rows in st st, beg with a K row.
- Next row: Cast on 3 sts, K to end. (7 sts)
- Next row: Cast on 3 sts, P to end. (10 sts)
- Work 24 rows in st st, beg with a K row.
- Next row: K2, M1, K3, M1, K3, M1, K2. (13 sts)
- Work 3 rows in st st, beg with a P row.
- Next row: K2, k2tog, K5, ssk, K2. (11 sts)
- Next row: P2tog, P7, p2tog. (9 sts)
- Cast off.

MAKING UP & DECORATING
Sew the body, arms and legs together as outlined in the instructions on page 17.

Use a separated strand of red yarn to work a row of chain stitch down the chest to make a 'wound'. Use a separated strand

of black yarn to work a series of short straight stitches across the wound.

Sew the head together as outlined in the general instructions on page 17, but stuff fairly lightly and do not close the top of the head at this stage. Fold the brain pocket lengthways, so that the right sides are together, and oversew the seams. Insert the pocket into the top of the head so that the seams are at the sides and the right side of the knitting is on the inside of the pocket. Oversew the pocket to the top of the head around the edges.

Place the two brain pieces right sides together and oversew around the edges, leaving a gap for turning and stuffing. Turn the brain right side out, stuff it and close the gap. Using mid-pink yarn, work a row of chain stitch up the centre of the piece, on both sides. Using mid-pink yarn, work a coiling shape of chain

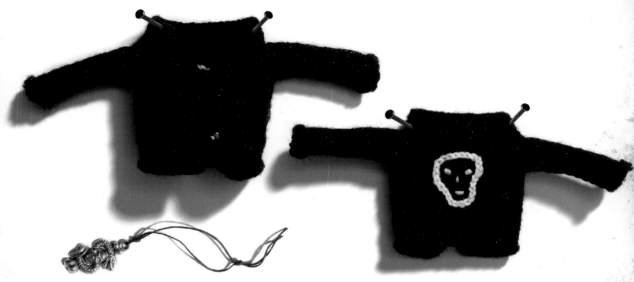

stitch along each half of the shape, on both sides of the piece.

Before sewing the features on the face, make sure the brain pocket is pulled out. Using black yarn, sew two French knots for the eyes. Work a semi-circle of chain stitches in white yarn under one French knot and in red yarn under the other. Work a straight stitch in black yarn across the top of each eye. Using mid-pink yarn, work five French knots on one cheek, wrapping the yarn just once around the needle instead of twice. Work the nose in chain stitch, using light beige yarn. Using black yarn, work the outline of the mouth in chain stitch and the centre of the mouth in satin stitch, keeping the stitches vertical. Using a separated strand of red yarn, work around one side of the mouth in chain stitch. Work two straight stitches in white and three straight stitches in green for the teeth.

Shade the eye sockets, using the grey crayon.

For the hair, cut eighteen 20-cm (8-in) lengths of fuzzy light brown yarn and six 20-cm (8-in) lengths of green yarn. Arrange them into six bunches, each with three lengths of brown and one length of green yarn. Space the bunches evenly around the rim of the head, securing them at the centre of the bunches.

Knot the skull and snake pendant charms onto the black waxed cord and then tie it around the doll's neck.

JACKET
MAKE 1
- Using 3 mm (US 2/3) needles, cast on 42 sts in sparkly black.
- K 2 rows.
- Next and every WS row: K2, P to last 2 sts, K2.
- Next RS row: K.

- Next RS row: K12, M1, K1, M1, K16, M1, K1, M1, K12. (46 sts)
- Next RS row: K.
- Next RS row: K.
- Next RS row: K13, M1, K1, M1, K18, M1, K1, M1, K13. (50 sts)
- Next RS row: K.
- Next RS row: K.
- Next RS row: K14, M1, K1, M1, K20, M1, K1, M1, K14. (54 sts)
- Next RS row: K.
- Next RS row: K.
- Next RS row: K16, turn and work on these 16 sts only, leaving rem sts on needle.
- Next row: P14, K2.
- Next row: K.
- Rep last 2 rows twice more.
- Break yarn and rejoin it to sts rem on needle on RS of work.
- Next row: K22, turn and work on these 22 sts only, leaving rem sts on needle.
- Work 6 rows in st st, beg with a P row.
- Break yarn and rejoin it to 16 sts rem on needle on RS of work.
- Next row: K.

- Next row: K2, P14.
- Next row: K.
- Rep these 2 rows twice more.
- Now work across all 54 sts.
- Next row: Cast off 3 sts, K12 (13 sts on needle incl st left from casting off), [k2tog] 4 times, K6, [ssk] 4 times, K to end. (43 sts)
- Next row: Cast off 3 sts, K to end. (40 sts)
- K 7 rows.
- Cast off.

SLEEVES
MAKE 2
- Using 3 mm (US 2/3) needles, cast on 14 sts in sparkly black.
- 1st row: K.
- Work 22 rows in st st, beg with a K row.
- Cast off.

MAKING UP
With the right sides of the jacket together, oversew the shoulder seams. Join the sleeve seams, using mattress stitch, then insert the sleeves into the jacket armholes and oversew them from the inside. On the reverse of the jacket, embroider a simple skull, using cream yarn. Work the outside in chain stitch. Work two French knots for the eyes and work straight stitches for the nose and mouth. Overlap the left border over the right border and sew on the small blue button.

TROUSERS
MAKE 1
- Using 3 mm (US 2/3) needles, cast on 20 sts in denim blue 4-ply for first leg.
- Work 10 rows in st st, beg with a K row.
- Next row: K3, cast off 4 sts, K to end.
  - Next row: P13, turn work and cast on 4 sts, turn back again and P to end.
- Work 6 rows in st st, beg with a K row.
- Break yarn and leave sts on needle.
- Cast on 20 sts for second leg.
  - Work 18 rows in st st, beg with a K row.

- Next row: K 20 sts from second leg, then 20 sts from first leg. (40 sts)
- Work 15 rows in st st, beg with a P row.
- Next row: [K2, P2] to end.
- Rep last row 3 times more.
- Cast off, keeping to the K2, P2 pattern.

MAKING UP
Using mattress stitch, join the back seam of the trousers so that the lowest part of the seam is level with the crotch. Join the inside leg seam of the first leg, again using mattress stitch. Join the top 4 rows of the second leg seam. Sew the chain to the waistband of the trousers.

BOOTS
MAKE 2
- Using 3 mm (US 2/3) needles, cast on 30 sts in dark brown.
- K 2 rows.
- Work 4 rows in st st, beg with a K row.
- Next row: K8, cast off 14 sts, K to end. (16 sts)
- Work 7 rows in st st, beg with a P row.
- Next row: P.
- Cast off pwise.

MAKING UP
Fold the pieces widthways, so that the right sides are together. Oversew the back, lower and upper seams, then turn the boots right side out. To make the hole in one of the boots, work a ring of chain stitch around the end of the boot. Trim away the knitting on the toe end of the boot and fray the edges a little.

Yoga ZOMbIE

**Zombie
Gravedigger head**

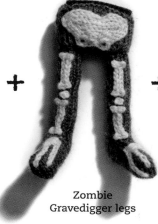

**Zombie
Gravedigger legs**

**Zombie
Gravedigger arms**

**Zombie
Gravedigger body**

**Zombie Cop
truncheon**

**The Mummy
grave bandage**

It's a gift to be simple – and there's nothing much simpler than Yoga Zombie. Easing his rattling bones into the full lotus position, he stares serenely ahead, though maggots writhe on his cheek. His turban is easily achieved with just a yard of grave bandage (see page 78) and a couple of pins to keep it in place, topped off by a femur he found lying around (experienced knitters may recognize Zombie Cop's truncheon). Ommmmm.

The MuMMY

All the zombies in this book are suitable for the mummified stained bandage treatment – so you can easily create two different zombie looks from one zombie knit.

PEDiGRee

1850 'Some Words with A Mummy', a short story by Edgar Allan Poe, offers a wry dialogue with a very sophisticated and eloquent Egyptian mummy.

1922 Howard Carter's discovery of the tomb of Tutankhamun, complete with the king's mummified body, kicks off a popular craze for all things Egyptian. Mummies begin to star in pulp novels and the seeds are sewn for the mummy's future in Hollywood.

It comes to life!

CARL LAEMMLE
presents

KARLOFF
THE UNCANNY in

The MUMMY

with
ZITA JOHANN
DAVID MANNERS
EDWARD VAN SLOAN
ARTHUR BYRON

A UNIVERSAL PICTURE

YOU WiLL NEED

121 m/132½ yd
(48 g/1¾ oz) white DK yarn

YOU WILL ALSO NEED
A pair of size 3 mm
(US 2/3) knitting needles
Red food colouring
A recently used tea bag or
some strong black tea

BANDAGE

• Cast on 6 sts in white.
• Beg with a K row, work in st st until strip measures 3 m (10 ft).
• Cast off.

MAKING UP

Sew in yarn ends. To give the bandage a bloodied, worn look, wipe on some undiluted red food colouring for the blood and splash on some strong black tea or dab the bandage with a damp used tea bag for the stains. The bandage is long enough to wrap the entire doll several times Wrap it around a couple of times to secure it at your starting point and tuck in the end when you have finished.

Index

ACKNOWLEDGEMENTS

The publisher would like to thank the following for permission to reproduce copyright material: p18: The Kobal Collection/Image 10; p26: The Kobal Collection/Universal; p32: The Kobal Collection/New Line; p40: Rex Features/Everett Collection; p64: Library of Congress, Washington, DC.; p70: Getty Images/Catherine McGann; p78: The Kobal Collection/Universal.

Genetic Counselling

A Psychological Approach

Christine Evans M.B., B.S., D.P.M., M.R.C.Psych.

Psychiatrist, Psychoanalytic Psychotherapist, Cardiff

CAMBR
UNIVERSIT

CAMBRIDGE UNIVERSITY PRESS
Cambridge, New York, Melbourne, Madrid, Cape Town, Singapore, São Paulo

CAMBRIDGE UNIVERSITY PRESS
The Edinburgh Building, Cambridge CB2 2RU, UK

Published in the United States of America by Cambridge University Press, New York

www.cambridge.org
Information on this title: www.cambridge.org/9780521672306

First published 2006

Printed in the United Kingdom at the University Press, Cambridge

A catalogue record for this publication is available from the British Library

Library of Congress Cataloguing in Publication data

ISBN-13 978-0-521-67230-6 paperback
ISBN-10 0-521-67230-9 paperback